PRAISE FOR *STEPPING OUT OF THE SHADOWS*

If you live in the liminal, meander the mysteries, are at home in the dark of the moon and in the wilds of your dreams, if you hear the Spirit of the Depths howling for lack of the Wisdom Traditions, you may be a medial. Your entrée to the uncanny, your sixth sense, are sorely needed in our fraught, transitional times. Yet sadly, medial women are often feared in our culture, scapegoated, ridiculed.

If this is your story, *Stepping Out of the Shadows* will be a gift to your soul and your spirit, an illumination of your sense of self, and a blessing on your life path. Roberta Corson has made a major contribution to Jungian psychology. Those of us who have lived in the shadows of mediality are grateful.

~Naomi Ruth Lowinsky, Ph.D., Jungian Analyst
Author of *The Motherline*, and *The Rabbi, the Goddess and Jung*

Roberta Corson has given us an offering of love. Honoring her teacher and mentor, Toni Wolf, she invites us on a journey to meet the medial woman; welcome her into our classrooms and therapy sessions; discover her in those we love; and even in our own selves. In this playful yet serious work, she tells stories, her own and those of others, that touch the untapped knowing that many women sense but have no language to express. She elegantly weaves theory, interviews, insights, and wisdom in a multilayered tapestry. This is groundbreaking work, offering a much-needed perspective for a world hungry for meaning and hope.

~Reverend, Dr. Sharon G, Thornton, Ph.D.
Professor Emerita, Andover Newton Theological School

Stepping Out of the Shadows is an inspiring journey into the realm of the medial woman. Roberta Corson shares her own story with honesty and vulnerability, allowing readers to connect to their own vulnerable truths. As I read it, I felt a new way of knowing open before me with a sense of richness, acceptance, and renewal. Dr. Corson brings forth the strength of the female medial experience from the shadows of judgment, ignorance, and misunderstanding. I can't wait to share this book with my medial clients and friends.

~Jane Cohn, LMFT, Depth Therapist

Roberta Corson's book feels like water in the desert for any medial soul who's lived a lonely life explaining and hiding their gifts away, rather than nourishing these gifts with the knowledge that they serve and support the world. It's a delight to read and re-read this book—the images, stories, and connections sparked recognition and resonance within my own mediality. Even before publication, I find myself adding names to a growing list of friends, colleagues, and clients who will receive this book as an invitation to explore an unnamed and perhaps unknown aspect of themselves.

~Nesita Kwan, LMFT, Depth Therapist

As an intuitive woman, I am so grateful to Dr. Corson for her labor of love in writing this articulate, well-documented, and heartfelt book.

~Mary C Culberson, Ph.D., Transpersonal Psychologist

Where has this book been all my life?!! It is a vital resource for anyone who hasn't had a name for the indwelling awareness that can be both gift and curse.

~Katherine Boyle, Founder, Veritas Literary Agency

STEPPING OUT OF THE SHADOWS

SHADOWS

NAMING AND CLAIMING THE MEDIAL WOMAN TODAY

ROBERTA BASSETT CORSON, PH.D.

Author's Note: All names have been changed with the exception of those in my family

Cover image: "Poem for a Six-Month Night"
Jeanie Tomanek www.jeanietomanek.com

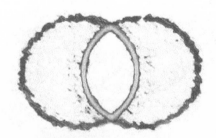

MANDORLA BOOKS
WWW.MANDORLABOOKS.COM

With gratitude to the copyright holders for their gracious permission to reprint excerpts from previously published material:

Reprinted with permission excerpts from Toni Wolff's *Structural Forms of the Feminine Psyche* translated by G. Jacobson in *Psychological Perspectives,* 1995.

Reprinted with permission excerpts from *The Witch and the Clown: Two Archetypes of Human Sexuality* by Ann Ulanov and Barry Ulanov, Chiron Publications, Asheville, North Carolina.

Reprinted with permission of the author excerpts from the chapter "Visionary" in *Meeting the Madwoman: Empowering the Feminine Spirit, Breaking through Fear and Destructive Patterns* by Linda Leonard, Bantam Books.

Special thanks to my friend, Gabrielle Heilek, for her personal translation of a line from Rilke's poem from the Duino Elegies, which are in the public domain.

DEDICATION

We are who we are
because of those who have gone before us,
whose love as well as wounds have shaped us.

We are who we are
because of the ones who have walked beside us
over the years and held us tenderly through it all.

We are who we are
because of those who follow us,
who move from the embrace of our arms
to embrace the world with their own

In this spirit,

I lovingly dedicate these pages to my family of origin
David, Lucile, Don, Lee, Bill

I lovingly dedicate this book to my husband
My Beloved Richard

I lovingly dedicate these thoughts to
Andrew and Alisa, our children
Matilda and Jonathan, their spouses
Nathan and Ashley, our grandchildren

TABLE OF CONTENTS

INVITATION

Are you a medial woman? How would you know if you are? Do you know a medial woman? If you met a medial woman on the street, would you recognize her as medial?

We are hiding all around, maybe next door or in the next cubicle. Since we don't wear name tags or carry banners and we look fairly ordinary, discovering who we are can be like unraveling a mystery.

Together we will be tracing the interlacing strands of a web that has existed in darkness, and as we shine a light on its different filaments, we will discover that they become translucent and reflect the many colors of mediality.

I hope you will come on the journey along this luminous web to delve into the mystery of medial women. Whether you are medial, wonder if you might be medial, love a medial woman, are a therapist or analyst who has a medial woman in your practice, or you are just curious, these pages will shine light on what has been hidden in your midst.

I've invited some medial women to join us as we move into this experience. As we tell stories and share dreams, active imagination, poetry, and reflections, you may shed a tear, crack a smile, or possibly laugh out loud.

The farther we move along this web and the more the light begins to shine through, I trust you will discover insights into what it is to be a medial woman. I have written these words in a non-linear style that reflects mediality. I hope you will find this journey enlightening, enrichening, and enjoyable.

Toni Wolff needs to be mentioned right here at the beginning of our journey into mediality, and I evoke her presence with us. Born in 1888 in Zurich, Switzerland, Toni Wolff was a Jungian analyst and close associate of C.G. Jung. I first met her as I read about her work many years ago. This was more than three decades after her death in

1950, but she was very much alive. As Wolff portrayed the medial woman, she touched me deeply. However, after I had written my paper on this for the class, I regret to say that I didn't stay in touch with Toni, though our lives were to reconnect.

I met her again ten years later in my doctoral program, when a male teacher lecturing on masculine archetypes disparaged Wolff's original work on feminine structural forms. As the *medial woman* is one of Wolff's four designated structural forms of the feminine psyche, I was incensed: how dare he! Immediately Toni Wolff rushed back into my consciousness, along with all she had meant to me.

As I began to process my anger and the intensity of my reaction to this man's comments, I received a vision of what my Ph.D. dissertation would be, as though it were a clear call from a deep mysterious presence. I would write about what it is to be a medial woman in mainstream Western culture; I would honor Toni Wolff. This came to me as whole cloth; every piece of it was clear, from the question to the process. I knew the moment of conception, and in the months that followed, and as I hesitantly began to speak aloud what I knew, it was like announcing a pregnancy.

And like a pregnancy, it developed and changed over time. The four and a half years that followed became a time of fleshing out the details, being still and listening, waiting, shaping, working, and imagining. It seemed like a long gestation, but I didn't have to drink tiger's milk or eat liver to make this baby healthy, as I did with my other pregnancies.

In this process, I fell in love with the medial archetype, for it has its own life, power, and sense of timing. We danced together during those years, this archetype and I. Then a few other medial women joined in, and then others who had studied and written helped guide the way.

Though this subject is anything but linear, writing a dissertation *is* a linear process. There are bones within each piece of the dissertation, crafted from culling, outlining, charting, and moving back and forth to convert volumes of raw material into a new whole.

There was loneliness in the process. I constantly realized that the work would not be complete unless I actually did it, for this was *my* work to bring into the world. Then just as suddenly as it was conceived, one night I said to my husband, "Oh my, I just finished my writing." I was surprised how suddenly the finish came. However, when the approvals began to come in, I was surprised at my sadness. It can't be over. These are the same feelings I experienced when my last child was born.

Fast forward several decades. In the intervening time, we celebrated my graduation; my supervisors signed off on the thousands of internship hours; I passed the licensing exams; I began my practice; the practice flourished; then came cancer and an abrupt retirement.

Through it all, my repetitive night dreams were that my encounter with Toni Wolff's work was an illusion, that my dissertation was not finished, that I still had months to go before I could complete it, and that I needed to get approval to write it, to extend the time, to find a new advisor, to go to a new school and write another one, that I was a fraud. Over the years, I had so many dreams about not having completed this work, that I finally put the dissertation under my bed, all 402 pages of it, so that any doubts that I had in the morning after one of these dreams could be assuaged by reaching down and touching it as it gathered dust.

In some ways, even on the night when I had come to the end of the writing, I knew that it wasn't completely finished. I had promised the Topic of Mediality that someday I would write of her in a medial rather than an academic way, in a playful way, in the way we had danced together, in a way that medial women could appreciate, and maybe even those who struggle to understand a medial woman at all could appreciate.

This writing has been a call; this has been a vision; this has been a labor; this has been a birth. It is bringing into this realm what has lived up to now in another realm.

What is it to give birth
    but to connect with the Other in love
        to long and wait and hope

What is it to give birth
    but to be open to mystery
        to become a vessel for unfolding
        to think throughout each day of what is within
        to know of a tiny heart beating its own beat

What is it to give birth

but to hold the hope of being adequate enough
    to pray for health
    to imagine, trust, wonder, and worry

What is it to give birth
   but to become a channel from one realm to the other
      to cry and laugh
      to work and push
      to believe in the future
      to feel the slick form slip from the dark
      to trust the unknown
      to love into life
      to release
      to allow

What is it to give birth
    but to mediate

NAMES MATTER

Once or twice in a lifetime, if one is fortunate and is listening, one hears one's own name called. This is an experience akin to falling in love, standing on a mountain peak, or holding your child for the first time. This is an experience of soul. It was just such an encounter that seeded this exploration, which is a work of soul. As you engage with me in this medial experience, I hope you will also hear your name called.

The ancient Hebrew tradition is that in naming, one calls forth an essence. It is no mistake that we named our daughter *Alisa*, which means "Joy" in Hebrew. She named her son *Nathan David*: "Son of God, Beloved." She named her daughter *Ashley Simone*: "Dream, Meant to Be Heard." Names matter.

For years the phrase, "there is no place for me," has pounded the interior of my being. It's an odd phrase, because to all observing eyes, there are many places for me. Through the years, however, I have continued to feel that I just don't quite fit with life in the world as it is structured around me.

Toni Wolff developed a theory that she called "The Structural Forms of the Feminine Psyche." She proposed four forms for women—*mother, amazon, hetaira* (lover) and *medial*. When I was introduced to Toni Wolff's theory of the structural forms of the feminine psyche and read her description of the medial woman, I heard my name spoken for the first time. As soon as I heard it, I understood immediately that I am a medial woman. I kept on listening, and, amazingly, the message has continued to reverberate in my soul through the years.

The feminine medial archetype is not understood or honored in our Western cultural order, and many medial women today unknowingly have made choices that have not served their medial nature. Some, like me, never knew their true nature until it was named. They survived by accepting other archetypes as their primary patterns of being, archetypes more acceptable to our contemporary culture such as mother, caregiver, spouse, lover, activist, warrior. Other medial women have moved to the interstices of society so that they may live their true identity freely, though they may feel like dandelions growing in the cracks of a sidewalk. Some have literally been tortured and cast out with the names "Weird, "Insane," or "Evil." There are countless unknown medial women who long to become who they truly are, but who have been bruised by cultural wariness of the irrational and mysterious. There are, however, many choices that medial women can consciously or unconsciously make between the extremes of abandoning their nature or living it at the edges of culture.

As our culture and the Earth experience distress, it is time to call the medial woman by her name out loud. To do so, one must look beneath the surface of the visible world and see through the eyes of the medial, which is what I hope to do here. This is the time to explore how a medial woman can live into the fullness of her essence. This is the time, in Rilke's words, "to hear the wind blowing the uninterrupted message formed from silence."[1]

And so, if *you* are a medial woman or wonder if you might be a medial, I invite you to come with me on this journey of naming and claiming. I also invite *you to come along with us if you love, live, or work with a medial woman and find yourself occasionally baffled by how she clicks*. I hope that you will gain an understanding of her, and maybe an appreciation too.

Most journeys have a path from beginning to end, which is somewhat direct. This book's journey is different, for it is a journey through "the web of mediality." This web moves in and out in many directions from the central point of mediality, with long and short strands that intersect and support each other. As we follow these strands, we will discover that some are sticky and uncomfortable, but since it is the medial who is spinning the web, she can be playful and insightful, and her web is quite beautiful. Together we shall venture into this web of mediality.

IT IS MY PLEASURE TO INTRODUCE YOU TO TONI WOLFF

Toni Wolff and I have become imaginal companions over time. She is a woman of many facets, some of which seem opposing. She has been described as "strict, disciplined, harsh, gaunt, haughty, forbidding, curt, intellectual, formal, elegant, warm, sympathetic, and insightful, and with a great air of something select and special about her."[2]

She has allowed me access not only to her writings but to her imaginal spirit voice, which is a bit different, for it comes through me. She is a woman who is the product of her time, and yet she is so much more. Recognizing that our era is more relaxed than hers was, she has allowed me to use her first name, Toni; however, in the Psychological Club in Zurich, she insisted on going by her formal title, "Miss Wolff." I invite her to tell you about herself through her spirit voice.

I was born in 1888 into a well-to-do family in Zurich and given every opportunity a girl could have. As a young woman, I enjoyed all that was beautiful, especially elegant shoes, and I spent time writing essays and poetry. This was the Victorian age, and my father was clear that women of our class should not matriculate into universities, as that would indicate to society that they could not support themselves without an education. My father's forbidding this was a great disappointment, as I loved to think and longed to learn. He wished for all his daughters a good marriage and motherhood. Though he was strict, he and I were close in many ways; he died when I was 21. He had put me in charge of running the household and caring for my mother and two younger sisters, as he saw me as the most capable. Of course, I did this and did it well, but I experienced pain beyond anything I could imagine at his death. You might now call it a major depression, but in my ignorance, I called out to the universe to know what was ahead for me.

I was able to get an appointment to work on this despair with C.G. Jung, the noted psychiatrist in Zurich, and we worked intensely together for some years. As I healed and we became close, he began to allow me to work with his life as his guide. I honed my intellect in relationship with Jung and the analytic community rather than at the university. I always regretted that I was not the doctor I could have been, if it weren't for my father.

A connection formed between Jung and me, as can happen when two people explore deep, dark places. This connection was different from others. He was married to Emma, and I knew he wouldn't leave her, but mostly the three of us worked it out. I became part of the family and had Sunday dinners with them. He and I spent Wednesdays alone at the stone tower he built at Bollingen. Emma was mother; I was hetaira, more commonly known as a lover. My love for Jung was intense. I suppose you would say I was his paramour, or his spiritual wife. His care toward me cooled later in life when he became interested in alchemy and turned his working attention to Marie-Louise von Franz. As I was increasingly alone after our relationship ended, I experienced great sadness, even anger. I wasn't even mentioned in *Memories, Dreams, Reflections*, which is an account of his life, of which I was indeed a significant part. I grew old, living a solitary life in the same home where I was raised. While this was heartbreaking, I also felt fulfilled, knowing that I had made my unique contribution through my analytic practice and writing. My deepest passion and greatest gift were working with my analysands.

Even though I always regretted that I wasn't permitted to be formally trained as a doctor, I developed a thriving private analytic practice, and Jung and I continued to work closely together for many years. I was part of the Psychological Club in Zurich, and it was to this group in 1934 that I first presented the paper conveying my ideas of the Structural Forms of the Feminine Psyche. Not much work had been done on the nature of women's psyche, so this was important for me to bring forward.[3]

Jung and I named and explored our understanding of the collective unconscious, which is the deepest layer of the human psyche and where all analytic psychologists work. This is deeper than the personal unconscious, which is contained by a person's individual life. The collective unconscious is common to all, and instead of being filled with events, relationships, and experiences, it contains "universally prevalent patterns and forces called 'archetypes' and 'instincts.'"[4] The archetype conveys energy that can only be encountered through image.

An American woman who followed me in the field, Ann Ulanov, along with her husband Barry, wrote these helpful words about archetypes, "There is no master list of archetypes, no fixed number, no sure way of discovering or identifying them. And yet we know when we are in their presence, or they are in ours. We feel ourselves linked to something primordial in its force, unmistakably authoritative, whether the force and the authority are those of wisdom or an intelligence best described as cunning. One clear thing is that it is a force in our lives, one with which we may absolutely identify ourselves, or from which we know we must struggle to disidentify."[5]

While my life was intertwined with Jung's and our work together was collaborative, my work on the feminine structural forms was my own. It has received much less attention than Jung's work; however, I have always believed it is as significant as his work. It is my work.

THE STRUCTURAL FORMS THROUGH TONI WOLFF'S EYES

While it would be tempting to explore Toni's theory in depth (as I have done in my dissertation and others have also done, including some entries in the bibliography of this book), that would derail our inquiry into the medial woman. However, before we begin to explore the medial form and what it is for us, I have invited Toni to continue to speak by giving a brief overview of her work and a characterization of each of her forms in her imaginal-spirit voice rather than her scholarly written words. She is present now and open to us as we begin our journey. Listen to her words.

> My theory, sketched in my lecture and paper, was based on the understanding that the unconscious structure in the psyche of women is made up of four distinct forms. I characterized each of these four natures by names: the mother, the hetaira (Greek word for companion, friend, lover), the amazon, and the medial woman.[6] Each of these is an image of an archetype.
>
> The whole structure I've envisioned might be expressed through the image of a web. The mother and the hetaira are attached by a thread of being "personally connected." They both relate to the external, conscious world, but in personal ways. The mother relates to the child; the hetaira relates to the man. The amazon and the medial are also linked together because the objects of their relationships are impersonal rather than personal. The amazon relates to the collective conscious, or the cultural contents of her time. The medial interacts with the collective unconscious, or all humankind's shared history

and memory.[7] It's significant to note that each form has both positive and negative aspects. Here is a graphic way to look at it:

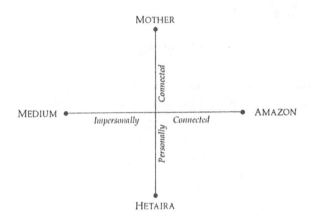

Usually, a woman is born with an identification with one or another of these forms, perhaps two that are side by side, again a bit of a web. She may discover three in her lifetime but probably has a hard time living out the third or the fourth form. I am medial but have also lived into the hetaira form easily in my relationship with Jung. It would have been almost impossible for me to have lived into the qualities of the amazon. There is a fluid development of these forms that follows a natural pattern in every woman, but it is important to note that the expression of these forms is conditioned by the culture in which each of us lives.

The Mother

The words that I think best describe the mother-form translate into the English words "caring, protective, supportive, giving, and instructive."[8] The mother is drawn to everything that is undeveloped, in need of protection, or in danger, and to anything that must be cared for and nurtured. The mother responds instinctively to what is unfinished and in need of assistance, and at her best, gives room for psychic development

and security. Fulfillment for the mother comes in her relationship with anyone needing protection, help, and development,
whom she then strengthens to the point where they can either
be released from her care or reap the benefits of the security
she provides.[9]

The Hetaira

The structural form of hetaira is opposite the mother and relates in a personal way, but not just to what's underdeveloped—
she can be characterized as a companion, particularly to a
man. She is intensely interested in the man's personal and
unique concerns, tendencies, and issues, and her energy is directed toward promoting these. She is drawn to the depths
and details of a relationship and leads him into his total personality. For the hetaira, relationships are decisive. Everything
else—social security, position, etc.—is irrelevant.[10]

The Amazon

The structural form of the amazon may be explained in words
and phrases such as self-contained, independent, interested in
objective achievement and fulfillment, competent, task-ori-
ented, undemanding, competitive, successful, and efficient.
Her great joy comes in self-expression, but she tends to dis-
sociate herself from her intuition.

The Medial

The fourth structural form is the medial, sometimes referred
to as *mediumistic,* or in the singular as a *mediatrix.* The word
medial means in between, neither one thing nor the other, in-
termediate, universal, neutral, in the middle, a means, an agent,
a mediator, a go-between. The medial woman is immersed in
the psychic atmosphere of her environment and the spirit of
her times, but above all, in the collective (impersonal) unconscious. The unconscious, once it is constellated and becomes
conscious, exerts an effect. The medial woman reinforces this
effect; she is absorbed and molded by it and often represents

it herself. For instance, she must express or act on what is "in the air," what the surrounding environment cannot or will not admit, but what is there nonetheless.[11]

I offer many thanks to Toni Wolff for these original and beautiful descriptions of her structural forms. Toni, we shall come back to you for more of your guidance later on our journey, for this is the path you created.

SEEING-THROUGH

There is a great difference between *looking-at* and *seeing-through*. The ability to see-through is what primarily distinguishes medial women from others, and all her other qualities follow from this. In the process of seeing-through, the medial woman learns what to look for and how to behold what she sees with imaginative eyes. Through this practice, the medial woman brings forth visions that cannot be seen when merely looking *at* something.

One of my dreams and the following active imagination speaks to this seeing-through quality.

> I am in a long school hallway. Someone points to a spider spinning a web in the middle of the hall. This is different from the usual web because the spider has spun different colors of the rainbow from the bottom up. She is now on red, and the spider herself is also now red. Like a Japanese lantern, the web is not flat but cylindrical and of varying diameters. I look through the web and suddenly see the hall through the eyes of the spider. What I see are dark, huge flies. The children at the end of the hall are light and blurry, but the flies are significant and move toward the web. I think, "How amazing to see as a spider does."

Active Imagination with Spider

After I had this dream, I engaged in a dialogue with Spider, a process C.G. Jung called "active imagination."

Me, the Dreamer: I do not see you, Spider. You have to be pointed out to me. I am not looking for life in this narrow and straight, straight and narrow hallway, with its precise, going-from-here-to-there, no-funny-business ambiance. The only life I see are children at the far end. This hall is the channel of the institution for children run by adults, the institution of rules and access into the adult world through which children must pass. I stopped expecting Creativity here when I was five or six or seven, when "bad children" were sent out to the hall all alone to "learn to behave," and when the whole class huddled there under our sweaters during atomic bomb drills, with visions of the worst horror a child could imagine. No, I did not look for you here in this hallway. Spider, Strange Spider, speak to me of your work and being.

Spider: I am more than you imagine. Every Spider is an amazing creature: coordination of eight legs, hanging in thin air from a thread, weaving, weaving, weaving webs of intricacy, beauty, and utility. Working and waiting, waiting and working. When my web is broken, I begin again. I spin to live. I live to spin. I know how to do this without words of training, without sterile hallways, without tests or papers, without well-taught rules. It comes from within.

But I am different from all other spiders. I come from the essence of light, the source of color. I am every shade and variation of the rainbow, the sign of hope. I am blue for sorrow, for the deep sea, and green for life, old and new. I am yellow and orange for warmth and red for fire, passion, anger, and energy. I am purple for peace and wisdom. What I spin is of my being. I become the color of what I spin; the color I spin is of me.

No longer do I work in two dimensions, but now in three. My web is a curved weaving: no beginning, no end; wide and narrow; long and short; anchored at top and bottom; running up and down, back and forth; every color sending light and impulse, yet each indistinguishable from the adjacent one. There is no one point where blue ends, where purple begins, and yet they do. My web is so unlike the hallway. Is it any wonder I choose to work here?

But you couldn't see this. You couldn't see me. Your eyes are trained to see square corners and long straight lines; however, you would do well to look upon me, to look through my web.

Me, the Dreamer: I do look upon you now and see the whole hallway through your eyes. The children are nearly invisible, but the flies are huge.

Spider: That's because I eat flies, not children.

THE WEB OF MEDIALITY

At this point, we'll pull together Wolff's brilliant sketch of the medial archetype with Spider's multi-colored, three-dimensional web and explore what we'll call "the web of mediality."

Indeed, mediality is a web. As one works to follow a single thread on a web, one quickly discovers that it's mysteriously interlaced with other threads. Soon what seemed to be a simple strand is seen as supported by other filaments and also supportive of the others. The image of the web cannot adequately hold the fullness of the medial archetype, but it can point to its qualities.

Let's look in detail at the nature of the medial archetype as it is expressed through women who have a strongly medial nature. I refer to "women" because of Wolff's original theory, but I believe the medial archetype actually includes men and children. Think of wise men or innocent children who seem to know mysterious things. In fact, I believe everyone has a "medial nature" to some degree that they could use whether or not they are strongly attached to this archetype. I hope someone will feel called to explore these additional dimensions of mediality.

Since Wolff offered the initial description and gave "medial" its name, my process of shining light on each thread begins with her reflections. It then includes other people who have written directly or indirectly of this archetype and have shone their lights from different angles. It would not only be impossible but also a great tragedy to untangle, crush, or demolish the web. The web of mediality needs simply to shimmer in the light of the early morning, the midday, and the late afternoon sun, as well as in the evening's moonglow. The purpose of what follows is to notice the shimmer.

Medial and *medialistic* come from the Latin word *medius*, which means "middle." Used as adjectives for a person, these words describe someone who stands in the middle and bridges two separate realms.

You may from time to time hear the word *mediatrix*, which means the same thing as mediumistic and medial. I prefer the word *medial*.

Irene Claremont de Castillejo, a British Jungian analyst trained under C.G. Jung, Emma Jung, and Toni Wolff, wrote about women's psychology. Her book, *Knowing Woman*, originally introduced me to Wolff's understanding of the medial and literally changed my life. As she described the medial process, she wrote, "To mediate is to be a connecting link between two things, . . . holding out a hand to each as it were, helping them come to terms."[12] A medial woman stands with a foot in each world and bridges the opposites, or she restores lost worlds to those who have forgotten these.[13] For the medial, one foot stands in the visible, tangible world and the other foot in the unseen, collective unconscious realm.

So now, let's gently follow some of the strands that make up the web of mediality.

Strands of the Intuitive

From my numerous interviews with medial women and my observations, there is a clear link between the medial archetype and the intuitive function as set forth in Jung's personality typology. The intuitive function points to how we take in or perceive what is around us. Those who are intuitive tend not to be as mindful of the material world, details, and concrete facts as their sensing counterparts are. Instead, people who are intuitive just seem to *know* what is not seen. They seek deeper meaning, are imaginative, and honor possibilities.

The link between the medial and the intuitive makes sense to me, and I suspect that it is the only one of Wolff's four structural archetypes that do in fact correlate with any of Jung's personality types. Phyllis Sherlock developed the Feminine Q-Sort, which enables women to identify their strongest structural forms. She then correlated the structural forms to Jung's personality types. Her study found that one hundred percent of women who identified as medial also identified as the intuitive type.[14] It is thus fair to speculate that all medial women are intuitive.

However, not all intuitive women are medial. Linda Leonard, an American Jungian analyst who has written extensively on women, creativity, spirituality, and life transitions, refers to the women whom Wolff calls the medial as "visionary." She speaks of the uniqueness of the intuitive quality of the visionary. While many women have intuitive experiences, the visionary's (and similarly, the medial's) intuitive experiences may be more esoteric, intense, and developed than those intuitive experiences of "normal" people.[15]

I've discovered that most people have no clue about the particular intuitive quality of a medial woman and easily dismiss or overlook it. So, it is heartening to read from Tad and Noreen Guzie, a Canadian couple who are an artist and a musician and who are also helpful guides along the way, that the "'sixth sense' is as natural to [a medial woman] as an ear for music or an eye for color is to someone else. With this realization, her particular way of *knowing* things, which had been a distraction and a burden all her life, now become a gift to be developed and no longer denied."[16]

Strands of the Elusive

The medial woman is difficult to identify in our culture for several reasons.

As Wolff recognized, there are few roles through which the medial archetype is comfortably expressed. So, it is usually kept hidden, and the medial woman consequently may end up living through an *acceptable* role rather than one true to her authentic self.

The medial woman is elusive because she frequently struggles to know who she actually is. In her permeability, the medial woman is in danger of losing her ego to that of another person or group. She may be completely unable to distinguish what are her own concerns and passions from those of another.[17]

It's difficult to discover a medial woman in the outside world partly because she tends to be inner-directed. As a medial, the woman is extremely sensitive to the intangibles in the atmosphere and will not succeed easily in pushing herself into external activity. She can bring others those things they do not sense themselves; she can be the *femme inspiratrice*, but she is not too likely to succeed in the business world.[18]

Strands of Social Context

Despite not naturally being a public person, the medial woman interacts with, and is shaped by, the particular social context in which she finds herself.

The general society often fears her when she conveys "what is in the air." Jungian analyst Mary Ann Mattoon, who has written extensively on dreams and Jungian theory, wrote that the medial woman expresses "vague and embryonic possibilities not acceptable to the dominant culture; that is, these women are sensitive to currents of thoughts and feelings not perceived by most people but which become apparent in the future. Because these contents are still unconscious to most people, they often appear to be dark, negative, and dangerous."[19]

Strands of Visions and Voices

The vision from the collective unconscious that the medial woman catches is but a glimpse of the mysterious whole. No matter how experienced, skilled, or developed the medial woman might be, she will rarely hear and translate the inner voice that comes from beneath consciousness accurately or objectively. However, she must persevere, for hers is an insight that needs to be honored.

Helen Luke was a British-born, Jungian-trained analyst who wrote extensively about women, aging, and dreams. She explored the necessity of persevering as we seek to hear the voice from the unconscious. "No one of us can hear the voice more than partially without his or her own unique re-creation, whatever its form, and quite irrespective of its merit or importance in the eyes of the many. All our efforts will seem inadequate: we fall again and again into mistakes, inertia or *hubris*, but it is the perseverance itself that will sharpen our hearing—not success or failure."[20]

Strands of Many Dimensions

A medial woman can never be described by one aspect of who she is. In fact, she has many, often contradictory qualities. Some of these include vulnerability, receptivity, the fear of going mad, loneliness, being misunderstood, the ability to live with paradox, and seeing the sacred in the ordinary.[21] In addition to these, she may experience feelings of reverence, feelings of difference from others, feelings of being caught in a tension between two kinds of reality, feelings of being helpful to others in the presence of death, and sometimes feeling unclear about whose interests and needs she is expressing.[22] She may also be inspirational, in tune with the new spirit of her age, swamped by the objective psyche, or confusing or destructive to others.[23]

Those who know her will describe her as internally complex.

Strands of Various Roles

Archetypes claim us. Try as we might, we cannot will them to do so, nor can we claim *them*. It is mysterious how the external situation in which we find ourselves combines with the collective unconscious, resulting in our discovering a particular role that either fits us or does not. Our satisfaction with a role comes when the role is grounded in the archetypal pattern most natural to us.

Throughout time and in contemporary Western culture, the medial woman has taken on various roles and functions that can fit her mediality. These include: actress, artist, astrologer, channeler, contemplative, counselor, creative spirit, creative writer, fortune teller, graphologist, healer, herbalist, hospice worker, creative marketer, magician, medium, minister, mystic, painter, poet, priestess, prophetess, psychic, saint, seeress, shaman, sibyl, sorceress, spiritualist, teacher, therapist, visionary, wise woman, and witch. There certainly are more.

From my perspective, based on the image of mediality as a web rather than a spectrum or hierarchy, there is an interweaving of the roles, which touch each other and yet lead off in different directions. For example, one artist may have shamanic abilities, or a teacher may be a healer. It seems to me that no one role is a purer expression of mediality than another.

Wolff named and defined the medial woman in a few paragraphs. However, the medial archetype is as ancient and complex as woman herself, appearing in many guises, displaying many moods, acting in every culture to some extent, given many names, and not easily found in its fullness in our rational Western world. Yet mediality remains and will find its way into women forever.

I AM A MEDIAL WOMAN

I shall invite you to meet some women from our own life and time as they share from the depths of their mediality, but before I introduce them to you, I would like you to know my own experience as a medial woman. You will come to see that each of us is different, and each of us shares qualities with the others.

I grew up in an intact, loving, intelligent family. I think everyone in the family except me was a sensing type, which in Jungian typology means they paid attention to data, details, and the present, measurable moment. Of course, I had no understanding of this while growing up; I just felt different and often somewhat stupid or out in left field looking at the birds, though I knew I wasn't really. What I share is in no way intended to be critical of my family of origin; instead it is to point to some of the inner struggles that I've come to understand through many years of analysis and living. I shall always be grateful for my mother, father, three younger brothers, and the family that we were and still are. I have been blessed.

The Stanford hills, which I roamed with family and friends as a child, and Fallen Leaf Lake, where my grandfather built a cabin in 1926, are "home" to me. My father was a doctor, and a professor at Stanford Medical School, and my mother was a Stanford nurse, turned homemaker when I was born. Following me into the family were three brothers. We all moved to Seattle from Palo Alto when I was fifteen. I went away to college in Wisconsin, majored in English, and then came to Berkeley to study for ministry in seminary. There I met, fell in love with, and married the man who sat next to me in Systematic Theology class. I can't say enough about who he is to me, but for starters, he is a healthy, loving, intuitive, compatible, faithful, intelligent, brilliant, poetic, spiritual, and competent person who loves me for who I am. We have worked together professionally in ministry until we both retired from the church. Together, we have raised two children, who are now loving, contributing adults, making this world a better place. Along the way, I undertook a year of training in hospital chaplaincy, earned a Ph.D. in clinical psychology, and had the joy of being a private practice therapist.

My native language is that of mystery, the holy, the irrational, the unconscious, and psyche. My family of origin didn't understand this language. My father was a practical man, a medical doctor, a man of the material world, a man with an outgoing and tender nature, a man of passion and compassion, probably an extroverted-sensing-feeling type, in Jungian typology. He was also a man with no particular faith upbringing and was uncomfortable with conversations about anything intangible. Yet, as an anatomist, he often marveled at the exquisite beauty, mystery, and intricacy of the human body. I remember how once he held up his hand with a sense of wonder and said, "I know every part of this hand: every muscle, every bone, every nerve, every tendon. What I don't know is how it all came together and came alive." The sense of awe with which he said this was probably as close as he got to speaking about God.

My mother was a highly rational woman whose father was Irish and stood firmly in the old-world traditional Irish Catholic faith. None of his religious teachings made sense to her, but she respected and feared him so much that she stayed in the Roman Catholic Church until she left home. It was not until her dying, as Alzheimer's Disease carried her back to a child-place and she spoke to me of her fears, that I realized how terrified of the God of the Irish Roman Catholic Church she really was. Though long ago she had become part of a liberal and loving United Church of Christ, the God of her childhood was vindictive, harsh, and apparently had always been with her in the background.

As a young child, I must have structured my psyche to mirror my mother's being, never realizing or developing a real sense of our differences, and I quickly banished my own yearnings, perhaps before I even knew they were there. Indeed, in many ways, I did develop as a different individual from her: I didn't like math, and she was a numerical whiz; I loved to read, and she rarely did; I enjoyed classical music, and she went to jazz; she loved the outdoors, and I liked being cozy inside; she thrived tending the garden, and I enjoyed cleaning the house. We recognized these differences, laughed at them, and usually honored them.

However, at a more fundamental level, I was not allowed much privacy; there were to be no secrets between us, and she carefully scrutinized me physically and emotionally. I shared everything with my mother, partly because I trusted her, and partly because I felt she expected it. She noticed every detail. This quality made her a great nurse, but it left me feeling that I was a "watched" child.

My relationship with my father's father, my grandfather Bassett, was significant in my early life and to my medial nature. I knew him well when I was a child because after my grandmother died when I was ten, he lived in a cottage behind our house and ate dinner with us each evening. A professor of speech and drama at Stanford, he was a witty, gentle spirit, grounded in the holy, which was not linked to denomination or form. He told stories of preaching to the chickens on the farm in Wisconsin when he was a boy. Perhaps he and I were the lone intuitives in our family, for he understood, affirmed, cautioned, and challenged me in a manner that others didn't. I attended Lawrence University, which he had attended, and I majored in English literature, probably because of his literary influence on my life. Apparently, he had an emotional breakdown as a young man, partway through Lawrence. He then journeyed to Southern California, where his brother lived, to clear his mind by working in the orange groves, walking up and down, down and up, tending the oranges. He recovered, went to Stanford soon after it opened as a university, then taught at Stanford. His life as I knew it, with sensitivity, wry humor, and spiritual grounding, has given me courage as I struggled with my inner forces, fears, and darkness.

My grandfather's spirit still lives in me at the cabin. I have realized over the years the mystical hold that this place has on me, not only with the remembrances of my family, but also with the depths, the heights, and the beauty of the universe that can be glimpsed from there. There have been tensions and sadness over the years related to the cabin, amid joyous times. Some of my happiest times there were when our grandchildren, the fifth generation at Fallen Leaf, claimed it as their own favorite place. When we decided to sell it, I struggled to release my hold on the deep, clear waters, the high, rough mountains, and the delicate, fragile beauty of the forests and flowers. Although I have now loosened my embrace on them, they didn't loosen theirs on me, and I have discovered that they continue to live in my inner realms. I learned that I no longer need to possess the cabin or anything else that brings joy. The joy lingers within.

My medial gifts tend to be inner, quiet, and subtle, so I do not stand out as unusual or medial, even if someone were to know that name. I also will add that I've had some experiences that are unusual, clear, and vivid, such as one which foreshadowed airplanes hitting the Twin Towers on 9/11.

It is God's presence that I tend most to mediate. Though I have been a pastor in the progressive mainline United Methodist churches, I believe that the God of Christianity is *only one* expression of the Holy, which has sought people and been sought by people through the millennia in every place on earth. From the time I was a child, I seemed to know the language of holy mysteries. Although others did not understand such mysteries in my childhood, my family obliged my longing, or perhaps pestering, and dropped me off at a nearby church for Sunday School, which was the only place I knew that spoke this strange language of mine.

I have had experiences of being fully in the presence of the holy and of being reassured of the larger dimensions of life in times of doubt and death. I have also had the experience of an energy that is not my own flowing through me in visions, ideas, and words. Usually, if I can have quietness and clear my being of the clutter of life, I can center and experience the presence of the Holy, which I can then mediate.

Dreams have been one of the vehicles of my connection with the realm beyond the worldly, for they have been a part of my life since childhood and often come with clarity. Some dreams seem to be visitations, whereas others offer guidance through human and animal figures or offer assistance in the form of unembodied images and words. Some of these dreams seem to come from the personal unconscious and some from the deeper mystery that enfolds all of life, which is the realm of the holy or God. Some of the most striking dreams are those that cross the boundaries of life and death and bring those who have died into my presence in a way that I experience them as actually here. They carry messages and assurances from beyond that rekindle our relationship. I cannot control or call up these dreams or experiences, but I perceive them as gifts from another realm, gifts to be trusted.

I have frequently had a clear sense of "knowing" the right direction, which isn't derived from information or reason. As a senior in high school, I absolutely *knew* that far-away Lawrence would be the right university for me. In those days, we didn't make college tours or even fly away to college, but only had catalogs with black and white pictures and long train trips back and forth. My husband and I *knew* on our first date that we would be married (he too is medial), almost before we knew each other, and more than half a century later, here we are! We almost instinctively *knew* how we could work together in our shared ministry, though we were the trailblazers among the first clergy-couple/co-pastors when even women ministers were rare, and we worked together for 35 years. I *knew* exactly the right time to try to have children, and what wonderful unique children came forth. I *knew* that I wanted to be a hospital chaplain or a therapist long before I could get the training or had the money or time to pursue either of these and sure enough, both of those specialties came to fruition. After a long and difficult search, I *knew* which house would be right for us and declared when the moving truck left and we closed the garage door at 10:30 on moving night that "We shall never relocate again!" We still have the same address. I *knew* that a place like Pacifica Graduate Institute was the right graduate school for me years before it was even formed, and I have my degree from there. I *knew* that whether I had life or death in front of me when I had a rare and aggressive cancer, it would be all right, and it was and is. Just *knowing* without any reasoning behind it. Just *knowing*.

Death has also been significant to the development of my mediality. My grandmother died when I was ten, and though I was not close to her, I remember walking through the park the day after her death and feeling the assurance of both God's presence and her presence. I wasn't invited to go to the funeral, so I created all kinds of negative images in my head. Shortly after her death, I experienced a terror of death along with chest pains and an overwhelming awareness that everyone, including my parents and me, would die. This panic quietly disappeared over time. However, my fear lingered that I would be called away from school, as my classmate Ruthie Sylvester had been one day at noon in fifth grade when her mother died; Ruthie was never to be seen by us again. I envisioned my mother or father in a casket and knew I could never say "goodbye" and go on without them. My child-soul was wracked with pain at the thought.

I was so terrorized during the atom bomb drills, in which we were taken into the school hallway and told to put our sweaters over our heads so we wouldn't be blinded, that I told myself I would *never* comply with those stupid rules when the bomb actually fell. Instead, I would bolt away and run home with my sweater over my head to be with my family, since I knew the way without having to see. If we were going to die, we would all die together.

Within days after I graduated from college and returned home, we discovered that Don, my 20-year-old brother, had a sarcoma in his leg that had already metastasized to his lungs. As a family, we spent weeks waiting, deciding, and struggling while he endured surgery, radiation, and chemotherapy.

During that same summer, my father became critically ill with a combination of rare biochemical diseases, underwent many delicate surgeries, received radical treatments, and gave the research scientists at the university hospitals new edges to their discoveries. Don died in November of 1965 at the age of 20, just four months after his cancer had been discovered. My father died exactly one year later; he was 52 years old.

A dream made a significant difference in how I dealt with the experience of my family dying. The day before this dream occurred, my father had been taken into the hospital for emergency surgery and was in critical condition. Since he was unable, I went with my mother to the oncologist to learn about the possibility of starting chemotherapy for my brother. In those days, there was no HIPAA; twenty-one rather than eighteen was the age of becoming an adult, and the medical profession thought they were protecting patients by not telling them much of anything. So, Don wasn't there for that consultation. "Cancer" was almost an unspoken word then. I believed then that we were all at the mercy of the knowledge and wisdom of these doctors.

Here's the dream.

My mother and I are sitting across a huge, shiny desk from an important doctor who has the power to cure all the ills of the family. We have deep trust in his authority and his decisions. Suddenly the room begins to spin around his desk, like a cyclone, faster and faster, and finally, it pours us out onto a wide street where the wind is blowing papers around. Many people are walking along the street, and everyone is pushing a push-broom, picking up the papers that fly into his or her path. I hear the words, "All you can do is push your own broom."

When I awoke, I knew then that there were no human authorities in whom to invest ultimate trust, and that we each have simply to push our own brooms, trust our own experience and authority, and live our own lives shoulder-to-shoulder with each other in the mystery of fly-ing debris. No one can understand and control the mysteries which blow in. I felt the necessity of "pushing my own broom," living my own life, trusting my instincts, and not attributing power and wisdom to that which is outside myself.

During this year of dying (1965-1966), I experienced many mo-ments of deep despair. In one of those, I went to the chapel of my church in the early evening to be alone with God and discovered that the church was locked. It had never occurred to me that a church would be locked, so I came home and quietly went around the side of the house where no one could see me and wept the anguish and des-olation of Gethsemane tears,[24] and Jesus' cry from the cross, "My God, my God, why have you forsaken me?"[25]

The dense writing and theology of Paul Tillich,[26] which I had de-voured intellectually in college, took on a powerful life of its own as I faced despair at the prospect of my loved ones' untimely deaths. I watched the foundations of my life that I had always counted on fall away: falling and falling until there was not much left. As I fell, I re-membered that Tillich referred to God as *"The Ground of all Being,"* the Being beneath being itself. When I plummeted, along with my whole life that was sinking, I landed on that deepest Ground, and surpris-ingly, calm came.

In his book, *The Courage to Be*,[27] Tillich claimed that the essential nature of courage is continuing "in spite of" all the brokenness of our existence and the anxiety of non-being and death itself. I made it through this horrible year by intentionally practicing the courage to be "in spite of" all that was broken, while staring death in the face.

During this time, I was haunted by the most challenging question for which no one really has the answer: what happens after time and life as we know it stops? Again, it was Tillich's sermon on *The Eternal Now*[28] that offered perspective. He wrote that there is *one* answer to this question—the eternal. There is no time *after* time, but there is eternity *above* time. Every moment of time reaches into the eternal. But sometimes, the eternal breaks powerfully into our consciousness and gives us the certainty of more than beginnings and endings. I needed to experience this sense of eternity in our midst and found the strength to continue daily.

On a cold November night, we all knew that death for my brother, Don, would come within hours. I stood with my father at the end of Don's bed as Don gasped for breath in the oxygen tent, and we said "goodbye" to him for the last time. As my father and I left the hospital arm-in-arm, he also in the process of facing his own death that would come within months, I experienced a deep and profound sense of peace, love, and connectedness that I knew was grounded in eternity and not restrained by the boundary of death. At that moment, I was no longer afraid of death for Don, for my father, or for me, and I knew that we would be joined in this love forever. Death, which felt like an impenetrable brick wall from this side, seemed suddenly like it might be a thin veil from The Other Side, or perhaps no veil at all. While I couldn't push through the bricks, I knew that Don could breathe into me through the veil, and I knew that love would move back and forth. I was surprised that I was able to release Don with serenity. This assurance of love and peace has continued with me at the core of my being through all these years.

Over the years, dreams that connect beyond death have brought visits with those I love. Although the people always appear embodied, they also can move through walls, or in one case, were sitting on a low wall right next to me. The most powerful dream was an encounter with my brother, Don, years after his death, a precious reunion with him.

I am at a beach home, ready to make dinner for my family. I walk into a small narrow kitchen and meet Don, who is already cooking in preparation for our arrival. I immediately hug him, but his body has no material substance in my arms, though it continues to be visible and appear normal. He tells me not to touch him. Then he tells me that he knew I wondered what happened to him after he died, and he said, "I just floated away from you, and it was gentle. Since then, I have been living with my children and my grandchildren." Then he crosses his forefinger over his middle finger and holds them facing outward to his lips.

His telling me not to touch him is reminiscent of the resurrected Christ in the Garden on Easter Sunday telling Mary of Magdala not to touch him.[29] Don's body, like Christ's, was real, and it was also not wholly material. I never doubted that Don's dying experience was one of peace, but I was surprised to learn that there was an unborn family with whom he connected, for he was only 20 years old when he died and had no children. There must be some quality that is ongoing and fruitful beyond death. At first, I understood his crossed fingers to say, "Don't tell what you have seen," and I held the secret of this dream for a long time. However, once as I described my relationship with him to a friend, I said, "We were this close," and then I realized that I had unconsciously crossed my fingers in the same way he had in the dream. So, it wasn't a secret; he was reaffirming our closeness. There are many levels on which such a dream may be understood; for me, this was undeniably an encounter with my brother, with whom I continue to feel close.

COMPANIONS ON THIS JOURNEY

Let's return to an earlier question: If you met a medial woman on the street, would you know that she is medial?

Medial women don't look different from any other women for the most part. However, interestingly enough, they may be quite different in some ways.

Before we proceed, I'd like to introduce you to a few of my medial friends, who will become companions on our journey into this web of mediality. Their stories have offered me personal insights into the life of mediality, and I trust they will for you as well. I have found it helpful to know that I'm not alone on this path of discovery.

As I was researching for my dissertation, *The Wounds of Medial Women in Contemporary Western Culture,* I requested referrals for medial women from trusted therapists and pastors. As part of the discernment process and in preparation for five hour-long interviews each, I asked each woman to complete Sherlock's F-Q Card Sort,[30] which could help her determine which feminine structural form best fit her. In addition to this, I provided some writing that described mediality. Ultimately, they then self-selected themselves as medial women. I transcribed and edited all the interviews for the dissertation. Now in the spirit Spider's colorful, circular web, I have woven together the story of mediality for each one.

I encourage you to imagine a portrait gallery with four women's unique faces and spirits encircled in beautiful oval frames. Visualize each one in turn as she comes alive and shares who she is as a medial woman.

These women will show up again and again as we journey together; they are both guides and trekkers.

Angela

I'm Angela, a medial woman. I had never called myself "medial," but I have always been drawn wholly into what is holy and away from what I perceive to be the unbalanced reality of the world.

I am 46 years old and was born in a large city. My father was black and my mother was white, so within my very biological being, I am both/and, neither/nor, and a bridge between polarities; perhaps I'm physically medial as well as spiritually.

My mother could no longer be part of her church when she married a black man in 1951, a wound she always carried but one she did not want to interfere with my spiritual development. My maternal grandparents supported my attending church; when they didn't go, I could walk down to the Baptist church next door to my cousin's house.

I always felt separate and different from both sides of my family. After my parents divorced, my mother married a pedophile, a sexual deviant. The next seven years were pretty hellacious.

During this time, I went inside emotionally and read like a fiend, prayed, studied scripture, and talked to God, whom I couldn't believe had abandoned me and not taken this horrible person magically away. Finally, at age 16, after living with my biological father for a year, I had the wherewithal to say to my mother, "This is what your husband's been doing. I can't come home and live with you." I went to live with my grandma. I learned how to detach very well through those years of my abuse.

Without seeing this abuser again, he died of a rapidly progressing cancer. I remember crying over his coffin and having people around say, "Look how sad she is." I was not sad; rather, I was absolutely furious that he'd died before *I* could stab him to death. "You son of a bitch, you left before I could get you."

I believed that I would not live long; actually, I didn't expect to live to become 21. I was 17 when I went off to college. I married at 18, had my first child at 19, had my second at 21, my third at 23, and my fourth at 33. I lived longer than I expected.

Over the years, I have worked with troubled children and adolescents in many capacities. Currently, I work with adult women in a post-prison detention center. The richest relationships of my life are my friendships. I also relish the places in my life where I can touch people in their spirits and move them forward, perhaps by asking a question that deepens their awareness of themselves and God.

There are times when I just want to be in the Spirit in everything I do. I want to go to a place where everyone acknowledges that's where we are. At those times, anything outside that place is assaultive. That could be the phone ringing or the television news coming on.

I experience the same thing running my institution and being in charge of everyone. I *don't dislike* doing it when I'm there, when I'm doing it. Yet, there are days when it's an assault, when I can sit in the office, close the door, and cry that I'm there and not sitting on the beach and being quiet, just watching the waves crash and thinking about how big God is and how wonderful creation is. That's hard.

My family never closed off any of the thoughts, ideas, or dreams I had. If I had talked about them, my mother would have been absolutely open. There were no restrictions on my being free to be me. There were no judgments about me that I knew of. There was no shame in expressing myself in different ways.

My grandmother supported my spirituality. I was very afraid of what I'd heard people call *dark spirits*. I didn't think of them as light or dark, but these spirits were not nice. My grandmother would appease me by looking under the bed and in my closet before I went into the room at night and assuring me that there were always angels in the corners of my room. I believe she made sure there were *only* angels left in the room. My mother's mother was *always* present in my life.

My sense of my spirituality was interrupted when I was about nine. It wasn't until I was in midlife that I was able to hear that God actually didn't abandon me during those horrible years. Though I was always active in church, I was unaware that grace would be available for me, too, probably because of my anger at God.

I didn't know about the medial archetype being a strong part of myself during those years. However, when I started working, I discovered that I had some strange qualities within me that I could further for the good of the world. Some people along the way said, "I don't know what the *extra* is that you have; I don't understand what that piece is; I don't know how you get to these troubled kids like you do." They knew that there was something *beyond* the skill, but they couldn't name it. I learned not to name that for them because I wanted them to name it in ways that were comfortable for them.

I work from a place within myself that is beyond thinking and emotion. I have a deep sense of God's hand, presence, or knowing in my life. It's a deep inner knowing, a *"before you were born and while you were in the womb, God knew you"*—kind of knowledge. This shift incorporates the head and the heart but goes beyond that to touching another's spiritual soul, their essence. When I'm real, I come from this place, and people sense it as, "You were really there; you heard beyond what I said to you." However, it's not *my* ability; it is something moving through me.

I think the Third World is much more open to integrating the empirical, the intellectual, and the spiritual components of life. These are all wrapped into one; they relate to each other in a circular manner. For instance, it would be very strange to me for my African-American friends to react with disbelief or humor if I said, "I do not like the *feeling* of this place." There would be no question about that. They would respond, "Oh, really. Well maybe I really don't want to go there either."

I do have really good ego strength, so I tend to like to go to the top in a hierarchy. I also want to be in charge of what I am in charge of. However, I'm extremely nonauthoritarian. It's very difficult for my staff to know when I go from caring, sharing, and nurturing to "I want this done, and I want it now" because I express my expectations in the same gentle language. Nothing is linear for me; I generally think in circular patterns. However, I also believe that there are proper ways to do things; there are ethical ways to do things, and there are moral ways to do things. My decisions are clear, my judgments are clear, and my paperwork is done professionally and clearly. My colleagues trust what I do, but *me* they don't understand. They approach me with a kind of suspiciousness.

I have known and trusted some people who were deep of spirit but became infatuated or entangled by the power of an administrative system. This has destroyed the relationship because there's no way I can be a bridge to the inflated power of an institution. Trying to relate to people caught in that kind of power robs energy vital to me.

I work hard to nurture my medial quality. I'm in therapy every week, so my therapist will hear all about what happens in my institutions. My personal philosophy about therapy is that I don't go to therapy because I have something wrong; rather I go because I *can't not* go. I have to continue to process my life and work through who I am, and it feels almost like a sin not to be purposeful about the work I do in both my conscious and unconscious life. Being in therapy is a chosen lifestyle. And my therapist is a bit like my guardian angel.

Speaking of such, a guardian angel is someone who just simply holds you, doesn't interfere, and can't stop you from doing something. S/he becomes a tingle in your ear or gives you a shake. How an angel communicates can be very, very, very, very subtle. The angel asks questions just to help you remember what is true. That truth is the truth that God knows, not that the world knows. Also, you know that God knows because you have that truth within yourself, and the guardian angel just protects that place, its sanctity.

I appreciate ritual, especially if the spirit is in it. I need things ritualistically attached, such as absolution, grace, or the spoken word. Historically we've lost and shut off much of the power of ritual. I'm bothered by some rituals that are simply rituals for ritual's sake, with no meat to them, not a breath of God anywhere within.

I renew my soul in nature as well. I have to have enough time alone at the beach or in the mountains to be able to come back and do what I need to do. I don't think God calls me to stay on the beach forever, but I need to be on the beach to hear God and be replenished. The problem is that I rarely have enough such time.

Mediality affects my relationships. I tend to be the giver more than the receiver in relationships. This was true even as a child. My mother was depressed after her divorce when I was seven, and I took on a parenting role in protecting her from that depression. I think I was not only dealing with my own problems but also was carrying her burdens. Later, part of my stepfather's threat was that if I told my mother what he was doing to me, he would punish her. I didn't tell her for many years. I also made a very conscious choice never to tell my biological father what my stepfather did. The overwhelming reason was that my father would kill him; there was not a doubt in my mind that this would happen, and I didn't want to risk losing my father or getting him into trouble. I didn't know much about prison then, but I knew he would be in trouble, and that would be horrendous.

My staff longs to be seen at a deeper level. I go in a little early on Monday to listen to each of them. There are many early morning knocks on my door and requests just to touch in and to become grounded before work. It's like they are saying, "I just need to touch you." I think it's "Angela's Spirit" they seek, so I say, "Okay, come on in." My staff is appreciative as well as loyal and protective of me.

I can be in that deep center in myself and trust myself to be there for other people, but I cannot trust many people to be there for me at that place. I'm very clear about who is available for that part of my being, with whom that part of my being would be safe, and where I might be nurtured and sustained. There are only a few people whom I trust with my soul.

I have a good friend with whom I have shared my new learning about mediality. She often calls me up when she needs a response to one of her problems. When she found out I was in this research on mediality, her response was to acknowledge this quality in me. She said, "I always knew you didn't just think up these answers, but I didn't know what to call it."

Underneath the trust of these few people is my fear that they will abandon me. It takes a long time to develop relationships. I have been abandoned many times, and when it was someone I've trusted, it felt like an annihilation. It was grievous. There were days, weeks, and months when I was a shell. I felt like my muscles were dripping, my tendons were rubberized, and nothing was holding me together.

I am a person of blurred boundaries. People don't know from where I come. People have asked me, "What tribe do you claim?" meaning Jewish tribe. People have thought I was Italian. They've thought I was Puerto Rican. I can actually disappear from a room; I'm not a person who would stand out; I'm not threatening. My coloration is such that they can't put me into a racial or national box. I have the ability to be what they need at the moment and not have to be conscious of it. I unconsciously take on the accent and the gestures of whomever I'm with. The habit is an automatic outpouring of myself into the other, and occasionally it's embarrassing or has caused trouble. I have no problem being in the skin of another person.

I've had a lot of illnesses in my life. I am very in tune with how my physical condition is connected to my psyche. One of my children went through an experience that was so painful for me that I could not get out of bed. I had such an intense asthma attack that I ended up in the hospital. What happened was so absolutely grievous to my spirit that I couldn't breathe. I never developed asthma until I was over 30. My kids got older; they're out there, and I'm still holding my breath. My therapist says, "Just breathe, okay." I know there's power in touch, but I tend to be very rigid. I really hold myself together to be here in this world. I have real problems with sleep, and I'm prone to ulcers.

I also want to share a few words about grace. I believe that God is always acting in our lives. The forces within me are somehow known, and they draw forces from beyond to meet them. God allows this. There is intention in the universe, a meeting of one's needs and apprehensions. The universe is created to be open to this, to hear this, and to provide for this. Often people don't believe or expect that what needs to happen will happen.

It has been a consistent experience in my life that I have always been given the next person who would allow me to explore the part of myself that needed to be explored next. The next person didn't have the answers. The next person couldn't lead me. The next person couldn't show me. The next person couldn't explain it. However, that next person could honor and allow me to explore my deep self, just where I was at the moment. There have been times when I have had to say, "I cannot go further in this without having someone new to do this with." And that next person would come to me in time.

There is a certain weight to being a medial woman, but it is a holy weight. I recognize the medial nature of my being not as a cross to bear but as a way of living, seeing, hearing, and filtering the world. I am responsible for giving the gift of my mediality to the world. To turn my back on this is to turn away from God, and that would be anathema. I am gifted and called as a medial woman. This is how I function; this is how I work. I need to be intentional, even if it means waiting. My life is grounded in grace.

Clelia

Hello, I'm Clelia. Though I was uncertain at first that I am medial, I can now claim this word as clearly descriptive of me. In fact, I find it very interesting.

I am currently retired, age 62, and live with my husband by the ocean. I'm a licensed clinical psychologist, a licensed marriage and family therapist, a speech therapist, and I worked in various administrative jobs in my younger days. I can't really claim one place as a childhood home because my family moved every few years, and I have lived on both coasts. My father was a government employee, my mother was a housewife, and I was an only child.

I had very different relationships with my two parents. My mother was an extroverted, kind, outgoing person. She was smart—people-smart, but not intellectual or street-smart. My father was quiet, an intellectual, a thinking type.

It felt like I had a foot in each of my parents' worlds. With my mother, I would be exposed to one kind of thing. When I was just with my father, it was different; we liked to go fishing together, or we'd sit and read books together. But it was very quiet, very quiet time. It felt good. So, I think I've got a little bit of both.

I have always loved fantasy and, as a child, could entertain myself for hours with make-believe. I spent a lot of time in my room playing anything I felt like playing. I still spend a lot of my time in a fantasy world, a world of daydreams in which everything can be the way I want to paint it. All this was accepted by my parents and not judged. I wasn't put down in any way, because they saw fantasy as part of a *child's* life but not something in which adults participate.

As a teenager, I wasn't particularly rebellious; well maybe I rebelled in the teeniest little ways, teeny little ways compared to what I realized later some teenagers were doing. I was a good girl. I always had a thing about not hurting someone else, even when I was young.

My love for fantasy found a place in high school and undergraduate school, where I did a lot of work in drama. I felt very much at home in the theater. However, my first husband was so linear that he couldn't see having a wife doing anything in the theater. He loved going to the theater but not having a wife in it. I just cut off a whole part of myself and spent years employed as a secretary and an administrative assistant. This worked for a while, and then it crashed. When my husband had the Ph.D., *his* Ph.D., and a job, I said, "Now *I* want to go to graduate school."

Administrative work was no longer satisfying, and I wanted to choose something more people-oriented. Something deep pulled me to go back to school and choose speech pathology, which was a great choice. I got a full scholarship to Stanford, so I went there, and from then on, I was with people rather than administration. I later switched to psychology, but I was still what my father called a "do-gooder." He said that our family had many do-gooders in it; it was a people-oriented family.

I left the business world to work with children. I realized that I loved working with children because I could go back to the world of fantasy again, which is the root of children's lives. The children I found who were the most fascinating were those with severe brain damage. These are children you initially can't touch, can't get near, and are unresponsive. I did a lot of sending them thoughts in the beginning stages. We were working beneath language because I believe that we communicate this way. I didn't have a lot of words for it at that time. I was just with them.

I always urged their parents not to remove their inner world but to make them bilingual. By *bilingual*, I don't mean verbally bilingual, but rather being able to function in this external world, which has certain behavior forms that are required, and at the same time to connect with their own inner world. I felt that their inner worlds, in which many of them were lost, were the very worlds that the rest of us are trying to mediate all the time so that we can get to this other quiet world. I think all children are generally in touch with the deeper realm. Somehow as we are born and come in from wherever we've been, far or not far, doing whatever we've been doing between times, I think we come in with a connection to the other world. But we quickly lose it; it gets taught out of us.

I had a more conscious experience of my uncomfortable relationship with linear reality while working for my clinical psychology license. When I finished my Ph.D. and was working for the hours required for licensing, I cut everything off from my psychic nature. Of course, I still used my intuition; every therapist has to use that. I knew my goal was the license and that these two were incompatible. I felt as though I had to operate only in the psychological world. It could have been that I was cut off from all that was medial in me, because I had so much to do to get the license, to stay in that world, to study for those exams, and to get all those hours. There are certain roles to play in the dissertation, in the internships, and in the exam in order to be a psychologist, so I had to cover up who I was. The process of getting the credential inflicted wounds on me. However, as we become more conscious, we learn to put up with some of the world's institutions because there is some good coming out of them.

My parents were brought up Catholic, but they didn't practice except Easter and Christmas. When you're Italian and Spanish, which I was with one parent of each, you just grow up in it. However, when I was about seven, I brought up to them that I wanted to go to church and I wanted to learn. They said, "Fine; we're not going to go with you." We lived near a Catholic church at that time, so I started going there for catechism, which I would take some afternoons after school. I had a lot of struggles with that because you have to memorize the answers. And I would say, "But why?" and the priest would say, "Just memorize it." There wasn't any discussion. I would go to church on Sunday; I would just walk down there by myself. Occasionally I went to some friends' churches, but I learned that somehow, I couldn't go to their churches because Catholics have this thing that it's not okay to go to any other church. That didn't feel good to me either, but I obeyed it.

I started reading about other religions, and we explored some of them in my first marriage. Then I just sort of put Catholicism aside for a while and got very angry. It's one way that separation can happen: you have to get angry. We spent time as Jehovah's Witnesses; we went door to door. That was very uncomfortable for me, door to door to door. It was awful. At some point, I got heavily into Eastern religions.

And then, after my first marriage was over, I began reading more about world religions and actually met my present husband at a conference on Religions of the World. My current husband is very different from me. He is a strong thinking type and is highly intuitive, with so little sensing that he doesn't seem to notice his environment much. We enjoy many of the same things, and our differences create growth and energy.

One night, I dreamed I needed to go to church, "because it is totally different now. I can go and love the church and the music and the beauty, and I'm no longer angry." When I woke up, I realized that something had been healed. I didn't have to hold on to my anger at the Catholic church. I could embrace it as well as everything else. I still did not buy the whole thing, but the anger was gone. I was peaceful. The healing may have been coming for a long time, but the dream just woke me up to it.

My husband and I go to all kinds of religious events and experiences. We go to talks by a woman who comes from the Hindu tradition, and I have a much more eclectic view now. I don't have a personal god, but rather it's an inner way. It's totally embracing. The true spiritual goes beneath all that is, beneath all the institutions. I have gone to the esoteric level instead of the exoteric level. The esoteric connects everybody, unlike the exoteric, which separates everybody with all these rules.

I'm retired, and my real focus now that I'm not "in the world," meaning that I'm not earning my living in the world, is with the spiritual. The Hindus speak of the third part of life as the spiritual time, for one no longer has *to make it* in the world. My longing now is for spiritual grounding and nurturing.

I am a very highly introverted intuitive type. I think what I primarily mediate is information. There are little inner voices, and I use them for my growth and knowledge. I've learned to trust the realm from where they come. What comes to me is often just a thought, just a feeling, just something, but it usually comes out and can help other people.

I know that there are many ways to mediate the realm beyond our understanding, and I've had experience with several of these different ways. My most common experience is with intuition or insight. Off and on, when the phone rings out of the blue, I'll get a flash of someone I haven't heard from and wasn't expecting to hear from, and it is that person. That intuition is just there, and I am trying to learn to listen to the flashes of intuition. However, if I am too hassled or if too many linear distractions are coming into my thoughts, these little things don't just pop in.

I can't claim profoundness. Some people can say, "Oh, I knew the instant somebody died," or "I knew the instant an accident happened." I don't think that I've had this experience. So often it's more that I think to call someone I've just been thinking about, and that person just happens to be down, depressed, and in need. My intuition is often about the small stuff.

I've had some other between-the-realm-experiences, which are not part of my usual routine but are more like little windows for me saying that "these experiences exist." It is as though I needed to know that they exist, but I am not able to turn them off and on. No matter how hard I work, it just doesn't happen.

I've had a couple of out-of-body experiences. In one, I was lying on my bed, and suddenly, I was aware that I was floating in the room, and I thought, "Oh, I'm out of body, and I'm floating." Then I started moving around the room and headed right for a bookcase. I said, "Oh no, don't bump into the bookcase because then I'll have to pick up all those books," and then I said, "No, no, no. Don't be silly, you're out of body; it won't hurt." I went right through the bookcase, just sort of right in. I thought, "This is incredible." Then I realized, "Oh Clelia, you forgot your glasses," because it seemed sort of fuzzy, and a little grayish, and a little dim. Then again, "Don't be silly, if you're out of your body, you don't need your glasses." I went through the doorway to the living room because I'd been in the bedroom, and just as I went through, my cat was walking into the bedroom. I was thinking, "Oh, don't bump into him," because I was going low, and I was going high, just going around. Then I went into the living room, just checking everything out, and I thought, "This is really pleasant, a little scary. But don't go out of the house." So, I didn't. I had some control. It was kind of scary, because I would think I would bump into something, but then I wouldn't bump it. That was very interesting. And then I thought, "Oh my God, I'm really out of body," and I got so excited about it. I said, "This is wonderful! This is so exciting!" The next thing I knew, I was back in my body. I was not dreaming. I knew the difference. It was not dreaming.

I feel like I've had these "hits," these windows of openness that say, "Here's something to know about." Yet they're not an ongoing part of my life; they are not something I can just call on and do. I've also had the thought that if I could do them any time, it could be a trap, for this is not what real spirituality is about. These are events, psychic events, powers of the mind, but they are not the ultimate thing. I could get fascinated; I could get stuck there; I could get stopped at that level. I think they're a piece of what happens, but they aren't the end. I don't know exactly what the end is, but I recognize these as side-effects of the spiritual development of the medial person. So, in some ways, I see how I could get really trapped in them if I'd had lots of them.

I'm not quite sure what to call this next experience, maybe clairvoyance. A friend had a theft in her home years ago. She came home and saw somebody was running out, so she went to check the bedroom. Jewelry was missing; some of it was old, and some that she had inherited, so it was very meaningful to her. She could tell what was gone, and she called the police. They came out and looked around, but they couldn't find any thief, and they couldn't find any jewelry. So, she said, "I'm going to call Clelia," because at that time, I was more active with this kind of stuff. The police told her to call, and they were right there when she called me. I responded, "Oh, my God, I've never done anything like that. Let me just get quiet and see if a picture comes. Then I'll call you back." So, I did, and then I saw a big white wall, a hedge, and the jewelry hanging in the hedge. I saw the sunlight sort of blinking on the wall. I didn't know what this meant. She had just moved, and I didn't know where her new house was, and it certainly didn't look like anything at her old house. I thought, "What the hell." And I called her up and said, "Look, I don't think I've got anything, but I'll just share what picture came into my mind. I see a big, tall, white wall and a hedge, and the jewelry looks like it was caught in the hedge, and some of it looks like it is on the ground, and there's some sort of sunlight on the wall, but it doesn't mean anything." She said, "It means something to me. That's the wall of the new place, and there is a hedge. We'll go right out." So, she and the police went out, and sure enough, the jewelry was there. I said, "I did that?"

I guess she must have told somebody, because a stranger called me and said she had lost a watch in her house. And I said, "*Nooo.* No way." My friend and I had a connection. I knew her, and we'd done a lot of work together, but I was not getting into the business of finding lost watches.

I decided that this wasn't going to be my thing. Yet, for a time I had worked with people as a sort of medium. These were friends, just friends that I knew. I would just sit down, go into this place, and they would talk to me and ask questions. I was an opening to guides. The image was that there were guides, or beings who were connected to the person, that I was channeling. Now where this was coming from, I don't know. Were other beings connected to these people who were using me as a channel? I don't know the structure. All I know is that I'd go into a trance-like spot, and I could hear information or get pictures, and then I would translate. The imagery is kind of vague. There is no sense of time with it, no timelines, no precise direction. The translation could be tricky. It always felt that there was some kind of other energy or being hanging around, so it wasn't just me, the personality, Clelia. I recognize that underneath there's a whole vast connection with others. The word *guide* persisted as a description, a name for what I was in touch with.

There have been times when I've just been flooded. One was when I began this channeling thing. It started with my suddenly being able to hear sounds or voices across the room; I was getting information about other people. I'd sometimes check it out and find out if it was right. It was just bizarre. Things were happening all the time. I felt like I was going crazy for a while, but I consoled myself by remembering that I was still functioning. The voices and visions were coming in. When it started happening, it was happening any place. I'd be sitting in a restaurant, and I'd have to hold on because so much information was coming in. It would disorient me, so I set up inner guidelines. Then I said to the voices, "You" (the You was this big sort of *You* that I didn't really understand), "don't do this to me here. Wait till we're home, and I'm in a safe space." It wasn't schizophrenia because I could then step back into the "real world," go to my job, do all those things. But I went through a period that was really disorienting. Then I realized, "I have boundary lines."

My body and psyche have an intimate connection. I think they pick up messages from each other. I've had some mysterious experiences of rapid healing that seem to have come to say to me that this *can* happen, that our psyches can affect our bodies. But I can't do this at will. These seem of the same nature as the out-of-body experiences: windows to show me that these things are possible, but they are not my way of life and are not in my control.

"Wounding" to me means to be separated from an essential part. I have pondered how *medial*, which means to connect, and *wounding*, which means to be separated, can go together. I think of all the ways I have cut off, covered up, or shut down something of my medial nature. My fantasy life has had to be secret as an adult. It was okay to have a fantasy life as a child; my parents didn't turn it off, but I had to keep it quiet once I was past that age. Somehow, I knew I was different, but I didn't bring it up. I think we have all learned to drop a little, teeny, tiny hint somewhere, and then when it is struck down somehow, we never show that part again.

In our culture, I believe that medial women cut themselves off from their best selves because they would go crazy trying to live in both worlds. Those who are archetypally medial but not conscious of it may be unable to verbalize or understand the nature of their struggle, so they particularly suffer.

I continue to make life-affirming choices, and the *new* continues to be born. Here is the story of my name, Clelia. I was confirmed in the Roman Catholic Church when I was about nine. I had to make the communion all by myself because for some reason, I was off-season from the confirmation of the other young people. My parents outfitted me in a beautiful white dress. The bishop was there to do the service, and I remember walking up a long church aisle all by myself, not even my own church. The church asks each confirmand to choose a confirmation name. I had chosen my Italian grandmother's name, Clelia. I loved her very much. The bishop said in his booming voice, "What is your name?" And I said, "Clelia." He responded in front of this whole church, "That's not appropriate! That's a pagan name!" I was shaken, stunned. I didn't say anything. He said again, "It's a pagan name! I will not allow that to be your name. You will be called Cecilia." It was a horrible experience! Clelia was the *real* name. My grandmother was a little angel; she was a wonderful, wonderful person, and I wanted to honor her. When I look back on it, the bishop was a real bastard.

For this research project, I was asked to choose a name other than my given name to be used. I chose Cecilia, my confirmation name. Upon hearing the story of why I chose to use the name "Cecilia" for this project, both my husband and the researcher said the same thing—"Are you sure that you shouldn't be Clelia? You could change your name back to Clelia." We did. The bishop's power trembles.

Elizabeth

I am Elizabeth, a medial woman. I am also a writer, a 38-year-old mother of two elementary-age daughters, and I am married to a self-employed contractor. Learning to see myself as a medial woman has brought me great relief, for now I have a name for who I am. I am beginning to have a new sense of myself as both real and powerful. I have felt that I've been different from others all my life but attributed it to other factors, such as laziness or a lack of being in touch. Throughout my life I've experienced pain and suffering, and now I can see how some of this is linked to my mediality. I worked in Jungian-based therapy for two years during a deep depression, but with or without therapy, I will always work deeply with the experience of my soul.

My family was somewhat traditional, for I was raised in the family culture of the '50s, though I was born in the '60s. My dad is a research biologist, and my mother is a homemaker who has worked for many years as a volunteer in the community. I'm the first born with two younger brothers. Although I always knew that I was different from the rest of my family, I have always felt close to them. The oldest of my brothers was killed in a plane crash in the cornfields of Iowa in 1989. He was the opposite of me in many ways. He enjoyed being out with people, although I have always been an introvert; he could set goals and accomplish them quickly, although I always seemed to be trudging through mud. As a child, I felt I should change how I was to become more like him. My younger brother is a great deal like me, but I think he fights it. He's married to a woman who is a completely conscious, "Type A," out-there person. She struggles with me. I think I threaten her, and I practice not being all-of-who-I-am around her. The Nike commercial is made for her—"Just Do It!" I need another commercial that says, "Just *Think* About It."

I always felt safe in my family. When I was eight, I was given a room of my own, and my family respected each other's closed doors. I needed the alone time that my room provided. My relationship with my mother was very special. After school each day, I came home and talked through my day with her. She became like a journal for me, a place to process thoughts, feeling, and events. I felt safe with my brothers and my dad as well. In fact, that processing continued into the dinner hour in front of the whole family; I had a high need to get everything out.

As a child, I didn't play the way other children did. I *did* play, but it wasn't the way they did. I was perhaps more serious than other children. My favorite activity was imagining scenarios or stories and dressing up. The table became our covered wagon. I loved it when the whole block decided we'd play Daniel Boone or some other roles.

The theater was one of my early paths not taken. In fifth grade, I tried out to be the princess for a play. When I wasn't selected, I was disheartened. Then my mother said, "Well, there are other roles. Why don't you try to be the witch?" I replied, "Ohh, I'm so disappointed; I want to be a princess." But she showed me how to be the witch in my real voice, my lower voice rather than my head voice; she showed me how to cackle from down deep. And so it was that I became not just a witch, but The Head Witch. And I was really good. Old friends even now at a reunion call out, "Hey, Old Witch!" The role stuck.

My body has carried part of my mediality, which showed up early in childhood and has been part of my wounding. As a child and teenager, I would build up a certain amount of stress and then become sick every two or three weeks. Though I was truly susceptible to allergies and whatever else was in the air, I remember that I just *had* to be home periodically. I just had to regroup before going out and being in the world again. To this day, I want the world to stop so I can catch up with everyone else. There is too much going on, too much to handle. Becoming ill was the only way I knew how to retreat when I was younger, but I discovered when I had children that you can't be sick and get away from parenting. You have to be really, really, really sick to get a day off from parenting.

It's a considerable effort for me to remember to take care of details and responsibilities. I realize that everyone in our family is affected by whether we live in a place of beauty or a place of chaos. Not everybody can live with the chaos as I can, so I am trying to accept my responsibility. It's really hard. It's as though my eyes are pointed in, and I just don't see the mess. I can tell the difference between physical beauty and chaos if I am really still and looking, but I don't always notice.

I'm a writer, a mom, a church member, a wife, a daughter-in-law, a daughter, a youth leader, a volunteer at school, a peer, and a friend. I know my mediality permeates all these. Mostly it is part of my writing. If I don't write, I'm not happy. I just have to write. It's not a choice.

I believe that the realm I mediate is the *unconscious*, to use Jung's term. Basements have been important to me in my dreams and in life. I remember the first time I rhymed something; I was in the basement next to the telephone, talking to my mom and playing a rhyming game that I'd learned. Then I made up a rhyme and gave it back to her, and I remember her saying, "Oh, that's a poem." Perhaps my call to the poetic comes from the basement of the unconscious, as my first poem came in our basement. I often dream of unused basements with unlocked doors and windows and other people's stuff. I need to make the basement my own, but it is so much work.

Psychic porousness is another medial quality that I possess. My ability to understand different perspectives and points of view doesn't mean that I agree with them or want to express myself that way, although my silence is sometimes seen as acquiescence. As a child, I could always understand this person's perspective, *and* mine, *and* somebody else's. Trying to be strong by either asserting myself or making a decision was, and still is, difficult. My mother recognized this and told me I should take an assertiveness-training course. I had to tell her, "Well Mom, *you* didn't teach me that; you taught me to empathize with the different perspectives."

Not having firm boundaries has always been a problem for me, so it has been really helpful to know that this may be part of what comes with the medial archetype. I sometimes have trouble distinguishing what is me from what is someone else, and I end up carrying or containing other people's feelings and experiences. I have carried my mother's depression and anxiety physically. I also carry group dynamics inside myself. When I come out of meetings, I'm always hyper and ready to volunteer for everything. I pick up on all the creative ideas, but I take them into myself, and then I *am* everything we have talked about. I just come out in a frenzy. I physically contain everything we talk about. Sometimes I'm so full I become physically ill. If this is so in a group, I wonder how much I pick up on things that are out there at large in the world. How many of my moods are affected by what's going on around me? How much of what I experience is my own, and how much belongs to someone else? I wonder if I will ever know.

I've always felt that the world is on a schedule and I'm not. Even as a writer, I feel I *should* be on a schedule. I struggle with the collective wisdom about the writing process that says, "Get your one project going; plan it through to the end; plan it; do it; work on it till you are done." It's all so linear. It's hard when my husband comes home and asks, "What did you do today?" I go nuts, even to myself. I just can't sit down and say, "I accomplished these ten tasks." And I've stopped telling him that I took a nap or didn't get anything done, because I found that this wasn't the truth. There was the dreaming, and the thinking, and all of those things. The schedule I probably should put myself on is an hour a day for daydreaming and an hour a day for writing.

I do need, however, to be honest about my own discomfort and my not understanding some of the other medial people, like the shaman, the healer, the psychic. Culturally we accept this version of the medial archetype, even though it's way out there, which seems as though that's the only way the culture accepts its expression. I am truly neither this nor that, if *this* means the mainstream culture and *that* means the psychic kind of medial. I'm glad to hear a definition of "medial" as more than healer, psychic, and therapist, because these are not who I am.

I've had my share of experiences with darkness, evil, fear, and trust. For me it began with the death of my brother in the plane crash. Then three months after my brother's violent and tragic death, we had a big earthquake. Did I ever feel that! My husband was gone to the baseball game; I was pregnant. I was really shifting, and it took me several years to stabilize. Physically and materially, I was so overwhelmed during that time that I could barely function. I could barely get the physical things of the day done. I could feed my kids and take care of them, but that's where all the piles of stuff in my house started to accumulate. I couldn't make decisions, and I couldn't go through things. I didn't believe I was really going to have a mental breakdown, but I knew I was right on the edge. When I've been there, I've been afraid *not* to look at it. It's dangerous, and we've had some women artists in modern times who showed us how not to end up, who couldn't handle it. But this dark chaos is part of what you get. This is part of the package. I always look at it from the artistic side, so it's not going away.

Although the darkness can have a deepening and strengthening effect, it can also open into evil. I have had one experience with evil which was more frightening than even the darkness of depression, because in it I felt a real danger. Looking back, it is a story whose main character was a woman who was a peer, a colleague, actually, the staff person for the community youth program in which I was volunteering.

Without going into details, I slowly began to understand that something in the relationship with her was using me up. At first, I thought I was volunteering too much. She certainly demanded that everyone work 110%. Part of my volunteering was that I was available to her on the phone. She called regularly and talked for an hour, and I would just listen to all that was going on for her.

When I finally wanted to assert some of what I thought, she reacted instantly and negatively. I realized that there was no room for what I thought in this relationship. I began to close off a small part of myself, but she was an intuitive person. She knew I was withholding something, and she reacted even more violently and worked against me, using individuals and the teenagers themselves to undermine and destroy me. I couldn't be myself with her, and yet I also couldn't hide myself. The minute I shifted gears from total support of her, the minute I put up a boundary to protect myself, she knew it. When I was no longer a totally open channel for her to manipulate, to use however she wanted, she became destructive, maneuvered others against me, and embodied a dark power. This may have been a place where my unconscious connected with her unconscious, which may be why it took so long to see. As I began to name the experience and go deeper and deeper, the dynamics became clearer.

I've had some dreams that speak to the fear of being invaded and taken over. One is of a house with an unused basement with doors and windows, which I am constantly checking because they keep coming unlocked. There is a threat that something dangerous is coming in. I've also dreamed about houses with dust all around, dust that comes in through shuttered doors. I recently dreamed that an evil sorcerer had sprinkled evil dust on Princess Diana and me to destroy us. I thought I'd swept it all out, but it kept coming in: swirling, evil, penetrating dust. I'm not sure what the danger is to me. It's something I haven't completely understood or felt right about in my self-understanding.

Interestingly, one of the things I fear most is publishing. I know that I have to write, and I know that I have to write for a big audience, but there's the element of danger. Once I've put a book out there, I and my thoughts are also out there. Then I've opened myself to whatever other archetypes and energies there are working as well. I'm very aware that there's a dangerous element that stalks people. Funny that this is what I keep focusing on instead of the women who might read what I write and say, "Oh, how was she able to look inside my own heart?" There is the backlash that happens within me and my own psyche as I contemplate publishing.

I also have a fear of being persecuted. Maybe I'm afraid of being known. Even though I may think that what I'm writing is "just a story," I also know that there are many layers to it. For example, we have the religious right in our country, which keeps track. I am literally fearful of them, afraid that they would find more things than I'd even think are in my writing. It's one thing to sit in my home and write, and it's another to take it out into the world and share it, especially when I have children and a family that are part of me, and whom I need to protect. I haven't begun to sift through my fears.

All that said, I want to conclude by sharing that despite my awareness of danger and my fears, I have a deep sense of trust. Trusting *people* may be the hardest because that's where I've gotten into trouble.

But I do it anyway. At a very deep level, I trust myself. I trust that I am a medial person, for though the name is new to me, it fits. Amid these interviews, I've had the experience of an incredible deepening, as though my gut were bottomless. Something needs a big space inside of me, and I trust my growing ability to contain it. I trust the vision that keeps coming to me, and the answers I've been given. I've learned to trust the darkness, which could be called hope or confidence. Somehow, I trust that I will get to The Other Side. I trust silence and can be in it for hours, but I can only *share* it if I truly trust the other person. I trust what is coming through me. It needs to come through me; it is trustworthy, though the place where I could put it is not always to be trusted. I trust that my writing will one day bring in an income.

I trust God. I've struggled with God, but I've never doubted that God was there to struggle with me. Trust always implies risk, but this is my responsibility. I trust the questions and the quest. I'm always asking questions; I'm always taking the journey. I very much trust the journey. I choose to use my gifts and be who I am.

Kathryn

I introduce myself as Kathryn. I am a medial woman, though I had never heard that word before, but my pastor recognized this in me and recommended me for this study. I am a channel for God's healing.

I was the seventh of seven children and spent some of my childhood on a ranch in Montana; my parents were in their 40s when I was born, people of good old pioneer values. My siblings were seven to 17 years older than I, so of course, someone was always telling me what to do. Two people often gave me the exact opposite instructions, which resulted in my becoming stubborn and independent in my thinking, perhaps to a fault. I had to be that way in order to survive all of these pseudo-adults with whom I lived.

My parents began their married life as homesteaders in 1917. My father only had a grammar-school education but encouraged and supported his children's education. My mother's high-school education was interrupted when her parents came to desolate Eastern Montana to homestead. My mother lost her hearing during the flu epidemic of 1918 and became nearly blind later in her life.

My father was philosophical but not religious. My mother didn't attend church because she couldn't hear. However, even as a child, I was drawn to attend church and went to various Protestant churches during my growing-up years. I later became active in the Presbyterian church as I sought spiritual teaching for our children.

Currently, I am 61 years old and am married to a wonderful man, a pharmaceutical consultant. We have two grown adopted children and two grandchildren. I was trained as a teacher and also worked in the area of personnel administration. I'm very organized and love people. When my husband and I were dating, we were aware that people turned to both of us with their problems, and we made a pact that we would do our best to help people. I knew *he* was a healer and also in a healing profession, but I never thought of myself in that way. Out of life's complications, I discovered my own healing gifts.

I have had formal training as a channel, which was similar to what one would receive in a graduate program, though of course no one recognizes this or even knows about it. It's very orderly and long-term. I have developed the skills of clairsentience, which means receiving feelings; clairaudience, which means receiving words; and clairvoyance, which means receiving pictures. I am what is known as a *subjective* receiver. Those who are *objective* clairaudients or clairvoyants see beings and hear voices. In contrast, I will have visions or hear voices that are equally clear, but they are in my mind instead of in the room. I also have learned body control for writing, drawing, and healing that comes from other beings working through me. My angels give me explanations telepathically.

I've been clairsentient all my life, which means that I can feel what another is feeling at a distance. One clairsentient experience happened when I was a child of about nine years old. I was going with my dad to bring in some livestock; my mother was alone on the cattle ranch, and while we were gone, I became aware that she was ill and told my father we needed to return. We went back and discovered that she had in fact tried to get someone's attention because she was having a hemorrhage from a nosebleed and nearly bled to death. In clairsentience, one cannot tell all the surrounding circumstances, but one can know the person's feelings at a distance.

I began daily meditation for my own renewal, and one day as I was sitting, my hands began to move. I knew I *could* control the movement, but I wasn't. I could stop it, but I wasn't directing it. This was when I discovered the spiritual gift of "control," where I allowed my body to be controlled for various reasons. One of the experiences of control is my "signal." I use this in counseling because it allows a person to communicate directly with my angels without me saying anything. When a direct "yes" or "no" question is asked of my angels, they pull on my ear: one pull means "no" and two pulls mean "yes." I also use control for automatic drawing and writing. In automatic writing, an angelic being actually controls my hand and writes a message or signs its name. In drawing, the angel moves my hand and creates a picture with the color and energy it wants. Automatic drawings actually take a long time to complete, often a couple of days, so I don't do much of this. After I finish, an explanation comes telepathically, interpreting the colors and forms in the picture.

As my meditation increased, so did my spiritual gifts and practices. I got into the practice of healing and then discovered that I was also a channel. In the past, I had not understood any of this, and suddenly I was trying to meet everyone's expectations, trying to heal the world, and I was about to crash. I know now how little *I* can do other than channel energy from beyond me.

I work in healing at all levels: spiritual, mental, emotional, and physical. They can't be separated. When I do healing work, I don't have to be in physical proximity to the person, nor do I even have to know the person. I can't say what really goes on here, but it's interesting to ponder. I know that in my imagination, I'm with the other person physically, though we are not geographically together. Somehow though I'm there in spirit, I'm also there physically. Maybe I am leaving my body. Perhaps I actually go. I don't know. I hear the request from the one who needs to be healed; I can see the diseased area of the body, and I just sit down and channel energy. I channel through my hands, and I use prayer. Healing is where my heart is.

When I began to reach a point where I found the experiences I had were valid, I had to acknowledge them as valid. This was difficult, and I tried to dismiss them as ridiculous. "This is absurd," I would say to myself, but then everything I do is absurd by cultural standards and values. However, there was something greater than myself working through me. Several times early in my work, I felt I wanted to quit, but I was compelled to do the work. Finally, I sat down and literally committed myself to God's service. I said, "I don't understand, but I will give the rest of my life to you, and I will trust that you will never let me harm anyone." I've never had reason to doubt this. It works, and as I've seen that it works, I can continue to be a source of healing energy with absolute faith.

My journey took me through several Protestant churches, but they didn't honor my work. So, I moved on to a church more in the New Age tradition that is open to people shunned by traditional religions and honors the gifts of the spirit. I was eventually ordained in this church. I value my relationship with this church and spent 17 years in its culture. However, I am at heart a more traditional person, and though I respect these people, I have different perspectives. For example, what a lot of people in New Age religions would consider spontaneous, I consider flaky. On the other hand, what I would consider well-organized, they would consider rigid. Those differences made it difficult for me to function in that setting. I'm not interested in the psychic phenomena prevalent in the New Age religions. My particular calling is to be ordinary and in that ordinariness, to bring awareness to others. My spiritual gifts are of no value unless they have an impact. I have returned to a mainline Protestant church, but I am *very careful* about what I do and speak.

Before I got into my role as a healing channel, I would hardly go into a hospital because as soon as I walked through the door, I could feel my energy leave, as though all the people and all the suffering were taking my energy. I would be exhausted. Now that I function as a channel, I can come out feeling much better than when I went in. This is because I've learned tools to use to channel *God's* energy instead of allowing people to take *my* energy.

It makes sense to me that healing energy is in the atmosphere's moisture. When I work in healing, I always pull with my left hand and work with my right. When I'm pulling, I'm magnetically pulling that energy. I've come to think that a way for people to cleanse their negative energy is to shower, to wash their hair. The running water will clear away that energy. When I get into a position of working with too many people, more than I can process, I get bladder infections. It's related to this same principle. It has to do with energy traveling through water. The moisture in the atmosphere sustains us.

Among the many ways I've been inspired, there is one that's particularly helpful to me. It is very, very simple, but I've tested it, and I feel it's valid. My angels simply call it "The Law of Good." It is this: one action in any situation will serve the highest good of all persons involved. One person is never sacrificed for another. This is especially helpful when I get to the point where I'm not coping and get weary of well-doing. I recognize that I have to nurture myself. If I begin to get into excessive emotional responsiveness, or if I get into feeling that I'm going to be physically ill, I recognize that I have to stop. I take the space I need, and I've found that no one sacrifices.

Some of my work is rather dramatic. I've worked with the police to find missing people. The biggest test I've been given came through the request of a mother of a pilot carrying several people in a small plane, which had been missing for nine days. My angels gave me the signal that I should participate in the search. I could track the plane to within one mountain of where it had crashed, but in the process, I had a lot of hard issues to deal with. For example, I was asked if anyone was alive, and I could determine that there was not. I had to ask whether the relatives really wanted that information. They wanted to know if the plane would be found, and I told them they would be contacted within three days. After this conversation, I went through agony, wondering about the impact on these lives if this information were not accurate. As I worked with this case, I was in the plane and saw the snow in front. It was a vision and sensing. I was there, and I could say that the workers were going to have a very difficult time, that they wouldn't be able to find it easily, and that they wouldn't be able to access it. All this did come to pass. I was told that there were no bodies in the plane, and then I went through the agony of asking myself, "What if they had parachuted out and were alive?" It turned out that they had all been thrown out. They were all dead.

I channel energy from This Side of Life, along with the angels working from The Other Side, to help a person who has died and is having a difficult transition. This is often necessary for young people or those who have had an unexpected or violent death. I learned how to do this from a teacher of mine. She was in close contact with a particular being on The Other Side named *Monal*. My teacher would physically go to an actual death site and work with Monal. The help, of course, is always on The Other Side, but when I have an indication that someone is having trouble with their transition, I go into meditation and mentally call out, "Monal, bring extra help from your side. I have a soul here who is having trouble with the transition." It seems that there also needs to be energy coming from the earth; it can't all be done from The Other Side. As this happens, the deceased one can then see the light, literally to see the light and go on.

I don't work a lot with dreams, but I have had some, which seemed almost like visitations in which my parents came after their deaths. Once, I was troubled about something, I don't remember exactly what, but I thought my husband was patting my hand. Then I became fully awake, and the patting went on, and I realized it wasn't my husband because he was several feet away on the other side of the bed. So, I said, "What was that? Who is that?" and I heard, "It's your mother. She's concerned for you."

I've been deeply wounded because of my medial nature, and since I'm an orderly person, I'll number these wounds as I name them.

First, from the time I initially discovered my gifts, people have had a range of responses to me, most of them negative. Some people consider me just ridiculous; some people think I'm crazy, literally. Some people are afraid that I'm evil. That really threw me. "How can you know that the devil isn't working through you?" people asked. This sort of thing is very, very difficult for me to cope with. I think people with gifts like mine are afraid of the things I've endured. They don't want people to think they're ridiculous, crazy, or evil, so they don't develop or use their gifts. On the other end, the negative responses are the responses that confuse *me* with The Source. These result in people expecting behaviors from me that I can't fulfill. They don't allow for my faults and weaknesses. I am expected to be more than human, which heaven knows I am not!

A second wound is my feeling that I don't really fit in very well with this earthly life. I kind of have a leg on one side of the fence and a leg on the other. I imagine that most medial women know that feeling. I need to get my expression out, but somehow, I don't need people to acknowledge me. I'm very uncomfortable with a lot of attention. I also resent materialism. I don't want *anything* unless I need it.

A third area of wounding for me is almost the opposite of not needing acknowledgment. It is the pain of not being recognized. There is much anguish in being called and then not easily finding comfortable avenues of expression for my gifts. I'm paid by the hour when I work professionally, but that isn't what I want to do. However, when I offer myself without fee or set appointments in a charitable way, I often am taken for granted and treated discourteously. That's painful, and it makes me think, "Do I have to charge fifty dollars an hour to be treated with courtesy and respect?"

A fourth wound, which is a sticky one, is that people become dependent on me. This is very uncomfortable. As a healer, it is essential for people not to become emotionally reliant on me and for me not to come between them and God. That's actually why I like the idea of being a channel between God and that person. The goal from the beginning is to set them free, for them to have their own relationship with God.

I've gone undercover, actually, which is a fifth area of wounding. When I was suddenly called, it was shocking that there was no openness for me in the traditional churches. Creative people need to create, and people who have been given gifts need to use these. If they don't, the energy becomes dammed up and stagnates, and they self-destruct. It is very painful not to have full access to who you are in the tradition in which you were raised. Very few people know what I'm about when I practice in my current church. There are many things that I could not even share with my own pastor, whom I trust deeply and who is a sensitive man. If I shared much of my experience with him, it could close his mind because it would be outside his own belief structure. In many ways, it is refreshing not to be known. One night after I had been in my pastor's morning Bible study class, I made a vow. I said to my husband, "It is so refreshing. Nobody in there knows anything about my real work, and I'm never going to tell anyone there what I'm doing."

A sixth wound is loneliness, which may be a result of being undercover, or may be just a part of the medial person's nature. It is difficult for me to share my experiences and the inner part of myself, even with people I deeply trust and respect. I've too often felt invalidated and discounted, even by people who don't know what I do and unwittingly say harsh and untrue things about the realms I work in.

A seventh wound that I carry is a sense of invasion and penetration because it is very hard for me to set boundaries. Part of it is that people expect me to have no boundaries. I have a lot of stress in some of my relationships because each person doesn't know that ten other people are calling me with their problems, and I reach the point of saturation. Even with people very close to me, I go to great lengths not to have phone conversations but rather to communicate through notes. It is a constant struggle not to get sucked into someone else's psyche. Part of the problem with boundaries is that I take too much responsibility; I do more than I should, and then I feel resentment.

I am deeply concerned, even afraid, that when I leave this life, little of what has been revealed to me will have gotten out. That's not from an ego point of view. My concern is whether I am doing what I came in to do because it is so difficult to find avenues of expression. I have a whole drawer full of books that are partway written, but I've only published two. It plagues me to think that when I leave this life, I may look back and think I did not do right by God for not getting this material out.

There is so much need in our world. I want to encourage people to reach out in love. I work in the ways that I know as a healing channel. However, it is not the tools that have importance; it is the love behind them that is the power. Anyone who expresses love is functioning as a healing channel. My angels have emphasized that all expressions of love are equally worthy and valuable. There is a great need in our world for love.

I am grateful that this study is being done. I feel affirmed by what I am learning and sense that this work may be directed toward a larger purpose.

Together

A medial woman may be found in many places, engaged in many undertakings in our society, some of which are congruent with her nature and some that seem far-fetched. It's hard to see how such women could be grouped together based on what they do. The medial women with whom I've worked and have known are all intelligent, educated, and competent people who contribute to the world at large. At one time or another, all have worked as administrators in institutions of various sorts: educational, corporate, religious, health, financial, and governmental. They are all committed to serving people and, if asked, will admit to caring deeply for people, the Earth, and all Creation. Given a choice, each would rather do what she loves than earn a large salary. In Jung's language of personality type, the women I know are all intuitive, which is one common factor of all medial women.

I.C. de Castillejo wrote that the medial woman is "not easy to discover, . . . and is not publicly recognized as having a definite role to play." The women I know confirm this observation. However, de Castillejo may be overstating when she reflected that they "seldom [appear] in public."[31] Most of these women have all shown up and been responsible in the social order, but they have not done so easily, nor have they been able to live their mediality freely in the world. Yet, they continue to be out in the world: mediating, adapting, coping, enduring, and offering their gifts. All of them make the institutions in which they participate run more smoothly, and none thrive in conflict situations.

As I have come to know diverse medial women, I have discovered that they seem to be of two types, which I have named the *subtle medial* and the *vivid medial*.

A *subtle medial woman* seems mysteriously to know and translate deeper realities that others miss. She generally is not recognized, honored, or clearly known by others, or perhaps even by herself. She may have characteristics that fit many medial roles but may not openly function from any.

Vivid medial women have these same qualities and may also experience clairvoyance (clear seeing), clairaudience (clear hearing), clairalience (clear smelling), clairsentience (clear feeling), and clairgustance (clear tasting).

Hollister Rand, a trained and respected medium, made further distinctions, which I find helpful. She spoke of the *psychic* as one who "interprets *energy* around people, places and things on Earth." A *medium* "is a person who receives verifiable information from spirits and conveys messages to people in the physical world." These spirits are those who have lived on Earth at some time. A *channeler* "receives *messages* from one or more spirit entities (some of whom may never have lived on Earth)."[32]

From whichever source a vivid medial woman receives information, she knows who she is. The public also knows who she is, and she functions in a distinct, recognizable way. Often this role is not understood and accepted, and as a result, she tends to live way off to the edge of the mainstream culture. She may be the psychic on the corner or the herbalist, who historically was branded a witch. Medial women who are *subtle* may sometimes have a burst of that which is *vivid*.

While medial women are generally not identifiable in the external world, be assured that there are many. One of my great joys is when a medial woman shows up in my life unexpectedly. I've found that medial women express colossal relief when I venture to call them by a name they haven't heard before. A medial woman always recognizes her name.

THE BEGINNINGS OF CLAIMING MY MEDIAL SELF

I now invite you into a drama where the medial archetype took hold of me through a dance with the mother archetype in a most unlikely place.

Prologue

"Hi," she calls out timidly from the family room as we walk into the house that Sunday noon. Braced for a burglar because the door has been opened, a wave of relief washes over me with her words. Of course! She has found a ride home from the university and surprises us with a few extra days before Thanksgiving. In an instant comes the motherly wondering: should she really be cutting those classes for a vacation of her own choosing? I am glad to see her, but my husband is on another track. "Are you all right?"

"Sit down," she tells us; her body is tinier, her face whiter than when she left excitedly for her freshman year, not two months ago. I am not prepared to hear this nightmare, which ends with "and then he took advantage of me."

"You mean he raped you," I hear myself saying. The words that follow have an eerie, rational, calm quality that doesn't connect with content or feelings. No, she didn't know him. He was big, probably six-foot-four. No, she couldn't scream. Yes, she went back to her dorm, was hysterical, wrote in her journal, went to the hospital, talked to the police, and vomited for hours. Large pieces of the story have vanished from her memory; details don't matter. A cold chill runs through my body. How can I get her clean? My baby! I feel a deep urge to scrub her through and through until every last bit of his invasion has vanished from her body and our memories. I need to make it all right.

Instead, we hold each other, we three, in the dim light of the November afternoon. We hold each other and weep.

Department One, Superior Court

Fast forward one year. I find myself in Department One of the County Superior Court, observing the trial of the rapist of my daughter.

I am here as her mother and am indeed in the grip of the mother archetype. Being a mother comes naturally to me. I ache a mother's ache and weep a mother's tears. Since she was not allowed to be in the court after her days of witnessing, I am here to listen and to tend to her being. That, at least, is why I think I am here; however, something unlikely happens, something dream-like.

What follows are reflections from that trial, which became the stage for a strange collaboration between the mother archetype and the medial archetype. In this life-taking setting, I gained a life-giving insight.

People recognize me as her literal mother in that courtroom, but it is the unseen medial archetype, which I alone experience, that allows me to stay here.

Soon I am in the grip of the medial archetype, as though the medial is offering herself to me. Were the mother alone dominating my psyche, I would be destroyed by the devastating humiliation and unfairness of this experience, but being balanced with the medial, there is actually grace in the midst. Through the medial archetype, I feel and see, experience and understand that which the mother would have missed in all the grief and rage of Demeter. The following reflections speak of this unexpected grace.

The landscape of this living dream is an odd one. The very environment shouts distance and separation of one being from another: high ceilings, tall draped windows, hard chairs, and barriers. Everyone has a physical and a functional place. The world is shut out, and from 9:00 a.m. to 4:30 p.m., one's employment, family, passions, and frayed edges are on hold in another realm, which has no relationship to this court. One's uniqueness is insignificant, unless it happens to be one's official moment to speak. The brightness of the day and activity of the street are shut out by heavy floor-to-ceiling orange velvet drapes, which are always drawn.

Shortly after arriving in this place, my glance wanders high up to the enormous Spanish-style beams bracing the ceiling above, and there I see painted Chinese images of cranes and dragons. "Odd," I think, but I look at them often during the following weeks and find deep peace in them, as though they are saying, "Be aware of the reality larger than what you experience here." Surely it is so, for the ancient Chinese symbols of Dragon and Crane stand for immortality. The artist who painted these beams in 1926 says to me nearly 70 years later, "There is something higher than the law." I doubt that this is what the judge would tell me, but I am grateful to have a deeper source of wisdom present at all times in this courtroom. I am now connected with a reality that moves beyond time and space, beyond events and passions, beyond culture and gender. This is the collective unconscious, represented in Cranes and Dragons.

My back aches. The chairs are torturing, but this is more than hard-chair-backache. I recognize this ache; my body memory tells me I have known it before. It resides in my lower back, which supports my female organs. Yes, the part that ached as our daughter was born 19 years ago, turned upside down in the process. This is back labor. Now again she is inverted and turning, pressing and being born into a newness I do not comprehend. Once again, I carry her within. My body knows what in life is deeply true even before my mind does. I carry within myself at this moment the birthing of a new era where women will be treated with justice, achieved through the anguished labor of confronting an unjust system. This ache is my child, is me, and is all women being born.

Each time I enter the courtroom, I consciously descend into the darkness to hold her soul in all its fullness so that the darkness doesn't eclipse her brightness. I struggle to hold the darkness and the light together so that fear and shame do not have the final word, so that the lightness of life is not airy. I hold within my spirit-body both her darkness and her light, her weakness and her power, her mistakes and her successes, her brokenness and her beauty. I hold, and I hope.

I listen and hear her name caustically called by the public defender; the sound stings my ears. My purpose now becomes to gather up the letters of her name as they are scathingly scattered from his lips, and before they drop into the dark abyss. I am filled with my daughter's name, carrying her sacredness within my soul. This is the time of protective in-gathering. The mother and medial archetypes work together now, each knowing and holding, each in her own way.

The courtroom smells stale. Someone opens a window and then closes it, the fresh air quickly lost in the harshness of negativity and the poison of evil. As a medial woman, I am endangered right now, for I am immersed in the psychic atmosphere of my environment, overcome by the dark powers that I feel to which others seem oblivious. The overwhelming forces of the collective unconscious sweep through my ego, and I am aware that it is weakening. I need to be protected from fragmentation and pressure, from the temptation to take in the public defender's blatant and false evidence. The forces are strong and consuming. I am vulnerable, far from those who love me, and alone for many weeks in this strange time and place. I have found a wooded setting where I go early in the mornings and late in the evenings. I sink my feet into the soil;

I fill my nostrils with orange blossom fragrance; I drink in the soft greens; I allow the warmth of the unused sun to fill me for the day or the coolness of the moon to still me for the night; I re-ground. As I walk among the trees and feel the goodness of creation, I remember that the courtroom, which seems so filled with vileness, is also part of this same creation, dampened with tears of anguish. I return to it again.

I look into this courtroom and see darkness, caused partly by dark furnishings, drawn drapes, and heavy colors, but these merely reflect the greater darkness of spirit and the closed atmosphere. I watch as intimidated witnesses shrink bodily under fierce questioning.

In response to the district attorney's protests to the judge in his chambers that he is not being fair and consistent in his rulings, the judge states clearly that fairness has nothing to do with this trial.

This certainly is his attitude as he presides over the trial: ruling with inconsistency, overruling the district attorney's objections when the public defender violates the limits even he has set, allowing the public defender to use literature in the closing arguments but ruling literature out of order in the closing of the prosecution, permitting days of character witnesses for the defense but none for the prosecution; granting the defendant's parents, who have observed the entire trial, to be witnesses, but dis-allowing me to speak to the veracity of my child, because I have been in the courtroom for the whole trial. The judge himself has said that this is "justice without fairness."

We need the presence of angels, beings of light spirit. Where are the angels? So, I start counting, and then I silently ask the angels to manifest themselves in the 83 candles of the chandeliers and the 12 recessed lights in the ceiling far above, and in the few light patterns that have deceived the orange drapes, made their way into the room, and are now playing on the carpet. One hundred angels have unmasked themselves and allowed me to experience them. I permit their lightness to play around those who need them. I now laugh at the pathos of this public defender who takes himself too seriously; he grabs the seat of his pants as he makes a ponderous point and scratches at the dark part of his anatomy, unaware. The angels made him do it, a trick of sorts, so I would know they are there. Perhaps this is one of the "techniques given to the angels along with arts, crafts, and cosmetic tricks."[33]

The public defender proclaims himself to be "Atticus Finch in the trial of a lifetime." He reveals his hubris in the pummeling of questions and the violation of physical and psychic space. He pounds question after question, raising inner defenses in the witnesses where there initially are none, presenting doubt when they are speaking truth, driving them into forgetfulness and contradiction when they have been clear. Even the sheriff's detective becomes intimidated to the point of tears on the second day of this attorney's attempts to undermine her integrity and competence.

The public defender penetrates my daughter's physical space by consistently approaching her without the judge's permission, standing next to her while asking questions, and at one point being so close that he marks her jacket with his pen. Obviously, both he and the judge (who overrules the objection to this behavior by the district attorney) are insensitive to Rape Trauma Syndrome, in which a rape victim experiences anxiety and panic when confronted with unexpected and unwanted physical closeness. Though the defendant has made a police-taped confession before the trial, the public defender now accuses my daughter of perpetrating the rape.

He breaches my daughter's privacy (and that of all writers) by waving her journal in the air, thumbing through it and quoting it out of context, and by walking the width of the courtroom, fluttering her underwear above his head and calling her "promiscuous." In the infinite, pounding repetition of questions and the disregard for the sanctity of physical and psychic space, my child is raped again.

I sit in the courtroom in the accepted social position of mother of the victim, a bit like mother of the bride. Everyone knows who and what that means, where one needs to sit, and how one should react. My child has been injured; I have been injured; *some* anger and tears are acceptable, as long as they are not disruptive, for I am The Mother. However, no one knows the other archetype that drives me as I sit there. No one knows the one who finds symbols of the unconscious on the ceiling, the one who holds darkness and light, the one who labors for the birth of a new era of justice for women, the one who struggles with being overcome by the forces of evil, the one who draws upon the presence and humor of nonhuman beings. No one knows. They would be hard-pressed to understand, for there is no place for me this in the courtroom. I am lonely.

I notice that courts are created with barriers: victim on one side, defendant on the other, judge high up. In my psyche, I push up against the barriers to focus on the whole. How many times during this year since the rape have I thought about and ached for the defendant's mother? Yes, her child has hurt my child. I am convinced of this in the depth of my being, and no matter what the jury decides, I feel rage. However, she hurts with her child. She did not want her son to do this and doesn't believe he has. I look at her across the courtroom aisle for days, moving out of her way as we pass, never speaking or exchanging glances. After several weeks, near the end of a morning break, I approach her in the hallway and meet her alone with these words, "I have carried you in my heart for a year, as a mother in pain." She responds, "I have thought about you as well. We have held you in our prayers. We have a connection, for we are Methodists too. My mother's father was also a Methodist minister." I respond by saying, "I don't regard you as an enemy or adversary but rather stand with you in the shared sadness of mothers. No one will win here." We return to our respective sides of the courtroom, never to speak again. My eyes fill with tears. This is "the place of soul, the neither/nor place,"[34] for we are neither friends nor enemies; we are neither winners nor losers; we are mothers in pain; we are connected.

In the fourth week of the trial, the judge becomes ill. The jury is dismissed for an indeterminate time period. The district attorney says that she will not accept a replacement judge, and if the presiding judge does not return, there will be a mistrial. I travel three hundred miles back home, haunted by the image that my child is now left indefinitely as a corpse twisting in the wind. She has been brutally battered; all the falsehood that could possibly be said of her has now been said. Will her memory be carried forever in those images left dangling in sounds splintering the air?

I long for a Joseph of Arimathea[35] to cut her down, to wrap her in linen, and to carry her gently to a borrowed, private tomb, protecting what remains from the hell of public spectacle. Von Franz stated, "In all civilizations the corpse is treated with great care and all kinds of rituals because it represents a mystery."[36] I doubt that this courtroom bears a resemblance to any such civilization.

The judge returns within a week, though he is clearly unwell. The trial resumes, and within a day it concludes. Joseph of Arimathea is not there. However, my husband, daughter, and I are there together, sitting in the front row for the closing arguments. My fingernails pierce my palms as I hear one last explosion of blasphemy from the public defender's mouth. I struggle to remain seated and not cry out in protest. My family holds each other and embraces soul in this darkness.

"We, the jury, find the defendant not guilty." The trial ends. The jury has reached its verdict. We drive north. She drives south. She stops eating. Over the next several years, I watch her balance between life and death on the razor edge of anorexia nervosa.

Conclusion

The end of the trial was not the end of our daughter's trials or our sadness. Yet, after struggling mightily for years, she has overcome much of the trauma of the rape, the trial, and anorexia: three violations in one. She did this through her inner strength and knowledge, her exceptional medical and psychological care, her strong relationship with family and the beloved man who was to become her husband, and by the grace of her own medial perspective. In the years since, she and her husband have created a healthy marriage and family that now includes their two teenagers. She is also a wise practicing psychotherapist and has been my muse as I have written this.

That month of the trial left me with one gift that I cherish. It was the beginning of my transition from identifying with the mother archetype to being claimed by the medial. Though I was clearly in the mother role in the courtroom, the medial archetype allowed me to be present and stay there. I wrote in my journal, "No one knows, and they would be hard-pressed to understand, for there is no place for me in this courtroom." And yet I was there. They saw the mother; I knew the medial. Both were at play there, and the two actually worked together, both powerful. However, they were not equal. I envisioned the medial as a basket that held the mother. As I allowed the mother role to be enfolded within the medial archetype, I found power and insight.

I know what it is to be claimed by the medial archetype, and I'll always cherish being my daughter's *medial* mother, as well as my mother's *medial* daughter. My soul tells me now that I no longer have to live the archetypal role of extroverted mother for anyone: for my own internalized mother, for my family, for the church, or for the world. I am a medial woman. Names matter.

TENDING SACRED FIRES

The night after the confessed rapist of my daughter was acquitted by the jury, I had this dream:

> I am looking for a Wise One and search up and down rocky cliffs and in and out of caves. It is bleak land. I come upon three fires at the entrance to a dark cave. I am afraid these fires will become out of control because my dream fires are usually wildfires. Then I notice that the first fire is held within a border of gold, and I know I can trust it. I also know that I am not alone, for someone has been here before me, tending the fires, and someone will come when I am gone. It is I who must tend them now in this barren landscape at the entrance to the dark cave.

I was alone for most of the trial, as it took place hundreds of miles away from my family and my supportive community. So, driving home on weekends to work in the church and then turning around and returning to that other town on Sunday nights left me tired and lonely. There was nothing familiar or comforting in this time and place, and the aloneness I experienced was immense. Indeed, it was barren and desolate.

Fires suggest passion, transformation, anger, and the potential for destruction. They call for both trust and caution. I am aware that anger boils again in my being as I write what I've long known: in the criminal justice system, there is little recourse for the victim. Twice during the length of the trial, wildfires broke out in different areas of the state. One necessitated the evacuation alerts of student housing at the university where my daughter had transferred. I recall coming from the court proceedings to my temporary, borrowed "home" in the evenings, watching the raging fires on television, and so much wanting to be with her. It was hard to find a place of psychic safety anywhere during those days.

Back to the dream.

I am searching in a bleak place for a wise guide, for Wisdom herself. I know that a wise one has been in this barren land because I recognize that not only have the fires been tended, but that one has also been contained in a circle of gold. The fire banded in gold hints at movement toward containment, completion, and wholeness, yet there are two that are not yet so framed. The barren wilderness paints the journey's loneliness and danger, and the dark cave points into the unconscious, to the unknown realm, perhaps to the mother, to the feminine, or maybe to death. The search for the wise one is then forgotten as I, the dreamer, take upon myself the task of tending the fires. I recognize myself as one in the line of those shamans, seers, poets, *curanderas*, witches, priestesses, prophets, and so many others who throughout time have been called to mind sacred fires, which is one of the tasks of a medial person.

This dream after the trial helped me accept my position in the long history of those medial ones who watch over the fires. The thoughts that follow are all part of my tending sacred fires in the lonely place at the entrance to the cave of the unconscious, the boundary of sacred space, the place inhabited by medial women.

Now, however, it is not quite so lonely, for as I tend these sacred fires, I know that others tend the sacred fires upon which they have come. We are coming to recognize each other, talk to each other, and teach each other. What a blessing to have Toni Wolff along with us, and the wisdom she offers.

ACTIVE IMAGINATION WITH TONI WOLFF

RC: Toni, I know you continue on this journey as a guide and that you are as delighted as I am to see how your idea of the feminine medial form is playing out in this time so removed from yours. By naming and witnessing it, we are helping keep it alive across time and spheres. I would appreciate another conversation with you in your imaginal-spirit-voice.

TW: I welcome the conversation. Time moves on, and I am honored that you know and value my work all these years later.

RC: So, help me a bit. My experience is that I was probably born trailing clouds of medial glory (to paraphrase Wordsworth)[37] but never found and freed my mediality until I read your words, and you named it for me. At that point in my life, I suffered profound anguish, because I no longer felt drawn by the mother archetype. It was all I had known, by name at least. I had grown up with it, assumed mothering was my duty, and knew it was expected as I performed my ministry. Actually, I don't know if I even thought about why I was suddenly unhappy. When I read your work, it felt as though my Intuitive Medial just pushed her way in and said, "No more, Mother, get out of the way. I belong in the front of the line!" And then I had to discover what it meant to be in my forties and finally come into who I really am with my medial leading the parade.

TW: A lot of confusion comes when we're born into a family or culture that prevents us from knowing our true Self. But when you did find yours, you allowed it to burst through.

RC: And then I had to figure out how to manage this new sense of myself, which had to do with mediating rather than serving. I felt totally lost.

TW: I empathize with you on that. Even though the medial is most important in enabling our culture to achieve greater consciousness, there is really no one clear way to do that. Every medial woman has to create her own methods.[38]

RC: It was only after a lot of anguish that my medial quality came forth, and I certainly didn't expect that to happen. I wonder whether it was my medial nature itself that forced open the very spaces that I needed to free it.

TW: The medial is a creative archetype. In your situation it bridged you away from being stuck in a past that no longer worked for you into the newness of a future that you took the risks to discover. When a woman is able to allow the laws of the psyche to unfold, she will become more conscious and return to the natural wisdom that has always been a part of her essence.[39]

RC: I appreciate that perspective; you seem to know about this. Have you experienced a situation like this where you had to live out of a structural form that wasn't really yours? Are you a medial woman? Or a hetaira?

TW: I am medial. That's why I intuitively went to Jung for analysis in the first place, why I was able to work with him through his darkest times, and why I was able to write this essay on the structural forms of the feminine psyche. But to be honest, I came to love Jung; we loved each other. In the Victorian age in Europe, the era in which we were both born, women were subservient to men. To stay connected to Jung, I intuitively developed my hetaira form. In many ways I sacrificed myself to allow him to come forth, in the name of the work and in the spirit of love. It was a costly sacrifice for his mark on history.

RC: My heart hurts for you in many ways as I have learned of your devotion to Jung and his keeping you in a secondary role and then ultimately abandoning you.

TW: I have had deep sorrows in my life, some of which I entered into willingly and some in which I was quite alone. I have never complained, though. My life was rich indeed.

RC: Your writing is quite linear. I don't associate that with the medial archetype.

TW: I am an intuitive thinking type. I wrote poetry as a young woman, but after I began to work with Jung, my thinking and writing were always subordinate to his. If I wanted to be heard in the society that I was part of, I needed to write like he did but in my own frame of thinking. As we talk, and I receive a glimpse into your era, I can see that the difference between the way women related to men then may be jarring to you.

RC: Truly. We live now in a time of gender fluidity, expansive roles, and feminine independence, though this is often threatened by those who fear. As I read about your structural forms, it seems that each form puts a woman in relationship with a man, but I wonder how you would approach that if you were to write now.

TW: If I were writing now, I would encourage each structural form to be defined in relationship with the woman's true self and all those around her. My culture was limited in this way, always consistently identifying a woman in relationship with a man; hence, so was my thinking at that time. It was a harsh limit on my life, but it was difficult to see it from inside that moment in history.

RC: And yet, look at the elegant, ground-breaking work you have given us.

TW: Jung influenced my work. He introduced me to archetypes and tended to use the concept of the quaternity, believing that the number four represents wholeness. As we worked closely together, that made sense to me. Our thinking was so connected that it was hard to consider that he wasn't part of my writing.

RC: As I think about feminine archetypes, I imagine they are much richer than four points on two axes. In fact, I believe that when one refers to archetypes, one takes off one's shoes, for this is holy ground, and holy ground defies our best definitions.

TW: One can never define or contain an archetype, only point toward it or experience it.

RC: I wonder what you would think of a different model, perhaps conceptualizing feminine archetypes as points on the circumference of a circle. Or maybe even as points in a sphere, which involves complex relationships that are beyond our human capacity to grasp. Perhaps they are like stars in the expanse of the universe without boundaries. Perhaps all women, all people, have access to a great variety of archetypal claims and encounters for which words about archetypes are simply descriptive rather than defining, and only partially descriptive at that.

TW: Archetypes and archetypal energy are so vast that speaking of them theoretically always distorts them. Archetypes are energy, and they expand as they are lived. For example, I have written about the medial archetype; you found my writing and identified with it; you allowed it into your being, and now you live from it, into its fullness that is unique to you. As you bring your work into the world, others will find it and live into their fullness in new ways. And yes, though I've been known to love beautiful shoes, this is indeed a time to stand barefoot.

RC: Being connected with you is such a privilege. You have helped me bridge your era and mine, your questions and mine. I am forever grateful for what you have given me. May you remain alive in what you have left for all women. I'm grateful that you are with us on this journey.

STRADDLING THE THRESHOLDS

In the universe there are things that are known,
and things that are unknown,
and in between them, there are doors.[40]

There are ordinary doors in everyone's life, and we recognize and often celebrate them: December 31-January 1; Solstice and Equinox; Friday-Saturday; today-tomorrow; births; birthdays; deaths. We don't know what is on The Other Side, but we pass through the doors regularly, usually with boldness or even forgetfulness.

Some doors, also called *thresholds* or *limens*, are the unique domain of the medial. These particular limens are often the most mysterious and unfamiliar. Picture many doors to many mysteries and medial people positioned with one foot on each side of a doorway. Sometimes, we don't really know what realm, whose voice, or what it is that we are mediating as we stand in the threshold. There are many liminal places between many deep realms, and our mediation varies depending on where we stand and what we are carrying across.

Other images beyond limen can be used to describe how the medial brings forth unconscious matter. At times we may find ourselves to be a bridge over a chasm. Sometimes, we are an open vessel through which there can be a flow. Interestingly, the image of bridge is dissimilar from that of channel. While bridge and open vessel are seemingly opposite, both relate to the task of connecting one realm with another. Though we may see ourselves differently and our roles may differ, the task is the same. What follows are some of the tasks to which we are called and what this requires of us.

To Mediate the Contents of the Collective Unconscious

Though the archetypal *nature* of the medial woman is immersion in the unconscious, the archetypal *task* is to bring the contents of the unconscious into the realm of consciousness. Our friend, Toni Wolff, has written that "the present contains within itself the past and the future. The light of consciousness rests on dark, unconscious seeds from which the objective cultural values have sprung (or will spring). It is this unconscious background that the *mediumistic* [medial] structure perceives. . . . [The medial woman] must express or act on what is 'in the air,' what the surrounding environment cannot or will not admit, but what is there nonetheless."[41]

To mediate the collective unconscious to the world of consciousness, a woman needs to have a strong presence of the medial archetype in her own personal make-up. She must "be able to discriminate between these two forms of consciousness. She needs to know which world she is in at any given moment. . . . She needs to know that one world cannot be expressed in the language of the other." The better she knows who and where she is, the more likely she will be able to bring across "pearls rather than chaos"[42] as she bridges the realms.

The mediumistic woman is "a receptive container for a flow of information that originates outside herself," as she helps others understand what they otherwise couldn't even see.[43] It is her task to express what she senses is going on under the surface of a group or event. The priority of the mediumistic woman is to mediate meaning in her unique way, whether or not it is understood or received.

This can be scary! And lonely!

To Give Birth to Images in the Realm of the Material and Literal

Artists are among those medial women who feel the impact of the extraordinary influx from the collective unconscious. Art, in its many forms, translates that which is beyond time into images: physical, visual, linguistic, and dramatic.

Russian poet Anna Akhmatova, a visionary and medial woman, said that "no matter how harsh the reality of the world, . . . escape is not the answer; the poet's purpose is to bear witness, embodying truth through the word."[44]

Images help in the exploration of the unconscious, for they give direction in confusion, speak the truth with a mask of secret knowledge, energize, and operate at a depth where rich but opposite truths are paradoxically valid.[45] The artistic medial woman witnesses Truth through imagery. Of course, this is one of the reasons that she isn't well-understood in this age of literalism.

All of us have some form of artistic ability deep inside. The father of my best childhood friend was a master pastel portrait artist. When I was about eight years old, my brothers, this best friend, and I began drawing portraits of each other in our backyard. Those were the days when we believed we could be and do anything, so of course, we showed them to her father. He took one look at my art and said, "Well, some people have it and some people don't." My portrait drawing days were over; my heart was crushed; I never held another pastel in my hand again.

I soon turned to music and learned I could convey much depth and feeling through my violin. I especially loved the Hungarian dances that my Hungarian teacher and I played together. They exuded color, vitality, and the essence of a culture I came to know through our music. I learned then that though we have different gifts, each gift is precious.

To Link Life and Death

One gift of the medial woman is her presence in the dying process, which is the ultimate bridge between existence and essence. My experiences with this embrace the most profound mysteries of my life.

The Spiritualist Movement of the 19th century, of which my great-great-grandparents, Andrew and Prudence Foster, were a part, believed that the dead wanted to communicate with the living and could do so through a medium who had special qualities that enabled this to happen. That was a cultural place for medial women of that era; perhaps my great-great-grandmother was a medial woman. I have no idea. From her picture, I surmise that she had no teeth, although there is no correlation.

Interestingly enough, during this same era in Switzerland, Jung wrote his dissertation, *On the Psychology and Pathology of So-Called Occult Phenomena*. The subject of his research was his cousin, Helena Preiswerk, who participated in seances, falling into a trance on the floor and channeling the words of the dead through their own voices. As a scientist, Jung did not admit to any personal relationship with her. He "omits his own participation in the séances, and dates them from 1899 to 1900, whereas they had started years before. Gerhard Wehr politely suggests that '[T]he doctoral candidate [Jung] was obviously at pains to conceal his own role, and especially his close kinship relationship, thus forestalling from the start any further critical inquiry that might have thrown the scientific validity of the entire work into question.' In other words, Jung the scientist thought it a good career move to obscure Jung the occultist's personal involvement in the business."[46]

Perhaps more contemporary and less esoteric is the ability of some medial people to be fully present and to guide a person through the final passage of death in this life to the mystery of another unknown realm. This can take the role of hospice worker, clergy, first responder, medical person, sensitive family member or friend. It requires an openness without fear, the ability to hold the entire range of feelings of the other person and oneself, and the trust that there is another side that is large and awaiting, though unknown. The experience of death is the ultimate limen known to us.

One medial woman's husband died recently. He was a man who was also close to me. In the weeks after his death, she and I both had dreams of him in which he was reaching out to speak about where he was and to communicate his closeness with us. For years they had meditated together every day, and she has continued to do this with his picture on the chair where he used to sit. She shared with me that she clearly feels his presence and experiences this as a new living phase of their relationship.

Another experience of standing at the limen of life and death occurred when I was training as a chaplain at UCSF. Actually, this limen was next to a bedside in the Intensive Care Unit where I was assigned.

A Holy Moment

I move between Mr. Jackson (an old black man with cane in hand, eyes full of tears, and words of faith on his lips), and his son, Kevin, who stands over his mother's bed in the Intensive Care Unit. Kevin kisses his mother's forehead and says to me, "She says she's tired. She waited until I was old enough to care for myself, but she's tired now." And then she dies. Kevin is eighteen...

As I sit in the chaplain's office across the street from the hospital that rainy afternoon after Mr. Jackson and Kevin have left, I reflect that the moment when a person dies is a holy moment, and the place where a person dies is holy ground. I wiggle my toes, damp from the rain, and I realize that I have slipped off my even wetter shoes.

The words from Exodus come back: "Put off your shoes from your feet, for the place on which you are standing is holy ground."[47] What a privilege to stand on holy ground, to be in a holy moment with strangers! What a privilege to witness the holy moment of death.

As a pastor and medial woman, I have often been privileged to witness the moment when a person moves from one realm into the other through the threshold of death. Though I could only physically stand on this side, my spirit could move across, if ever so briefly, and be with their lingering spirit. It is always a holy moment.

Today Sadie Died

Today
   Sadie
      died.

One-hundred-one years old
      and some weeks.

I come a few minutes late,
     only a few;
        she is still warm.

They let me in behind the curtain.
They hurry off with her possessions,
   Forgetting the spring picture.
        One-hundred-one years of life:
        one armload of belongings
           and a picture left behind.

They huddle at the desk—
 young, students perhaps.
   Have they ever seen death?
   Is their silence holding the mystery?

And I?
I go to keep her company.
 It isn't too late.
   Though her breath does not move,
   her spirit is here.

And we talk,
 As I hold her shriveled
     worn-out body.
I tell her I am here.
She says, "I knew you would come,"
 As she has said so many times before,
   Except this time, there are no words.

I bid her a good journey.
We say good-bye.

How often have we glimpsed the eternal
 through each other:
   She through me,
   I through her
     at the side of the bed.

How I wish I had written her precious insights
     Her wise statements:
 so simple
 so faithful
 so lost in my forgetfulness now.
Yet her essence is not lost.
Her essence is with me
   as she and I let her body go.

I hardly know her,
 Yet I have the holy task

Of embracing her in death
    After one-hundred-one years and some weeks
        of living
        of holding
        of being held.

She no longer needs her teeth
    or hearing aid or eye glasses.
She no longer needs her straight stature
    and dignified bearing.
She no longer needs the spring picture
    she painted when she was young.
    or the pink flowers embedded in plastic,
        which she somehow thought
        I had given her.

She leaves nearly as naked as she entered
        so long ago,
  with her now no-longer-new knees
    crinkled against her chest.

O Mystery of Death, whoever you are...
    are you not in part a mother on The Other Side:
      receiving her
        holding her
          loving her into new life?

To Carry Forth Butterflies from Ashes

Bridging this side and The Other Side of death is among the most expansive undertakings of the medial person. However, it means accompanying not just men, women, and children into their deaths but also institutions, organizations, and perhaps society itself as they all change and perhaps die. As I write this, I am aware of the ways that the church, as it is known, teeters on the edge of survival, of the questions about whether our democracy will survive, of the threat to life by the Covid pandemic, and of the immense dangers contained in global warming. Sometimes I feel despair, sometimes grief, always sadness at the thoughts of the demise of what has been precious.

However, the openness and hope that a medial person can bring to these transitions and losses is an antidote to fear that is so often experienced.

Here is a dream that visited me when I was a pastor many years ago. I was struggling at that time with my role as minister, though that local church was strong and healthy. Ironically, now that church is struggling, and I am strong and healthy. Such are the cycles of life. This dream came to me shortly after the East Bay fire that killed many people, and surely it was inspired by that event but seemingly had a life of its own. It lifted me and offered hope:

> I am walking down a country path with some colleagues and come to a monolithic Spanish-style monastery at the side of the road. It catches fire and burns to the ground immediately. The monks run out and stand safely with my colleagues at a distance. I go right into the middle of the ashes and discover a metal post. Attached to the post is a thread, and at the end of the thread is a tissue paper butterfly, which alone has survived the blaze. I take the butterfly and put it into a paper bag of belongings that I carry. As I leave, I notice that the butterfly carries so much heat that it has ignited a candle that I hold. I continue on my way.

To be honest, I have no idea what I would have done with the hot butterfly and burning candle in the paper bag of my dream, but I know the spark is alive and contained, and I am entrusted with it.

As I turn that dream over in my heart and mind, I am reminded of the trip that Elisabeth Kübler-Ross took into the concentration camp of Maidanek in Poland following World War II. After looking at tangled, fungus-covered masses of shoes and human hair piled into abandoned railroad cars, she walked into the shadows of the barracks. As her eyes adjusted to the darkness, what struck her was the graffiti on the walls. Hundreds of initials were carved into the wood along with pathetic messages, and among them were drawings of butterflies: scratchings of butterflies everywhere.[48] While she didn't know what it truly meant, she said this: "Within days, perhaps within hours of their dying in the gas chambers, the doomed men, women, and children had left their last messages—not of despair, but of hope, not of grief, but of conviction of freedom."[49]

As we look at the ways that there is pain, discouragement, despair, anxiety, or grief in our own lives, and when that which we thought was solid disintegrates before our eyes, it is the time to watch for butterflies, however improbable. The medial archetype helps us see them through the sorrow. May the miracle of their presence be the energy and light, the hope and freedom that will guide us on.

To Connect the Mundane with the Holy

One of my disappointments with some branches of depth psychology is that it doesn't go far enough in its understanding of meaning, for it envisions the unconscious as the ultimate realm within which all else is held. Before the language of depth psychology found me, I was claimed by the language of the Divine, actually from the very early age of three. As with the collective unconscious, one can only point toward or speak in images about the Divine. Unfortunately, these descriptions can become codified by the groups who share them. Through such rigidity, divisions are created, as well as essential mysteries diminished. All major religions are subject to this distortion of the Divine as they distill it into existence.

Yet, in its essence, that which is Holy is beyond the human psyche, beyond words, beyond images, beyond meaning. Its gift is that we can catch a partial glimpse now and then and be forever changed.

These beautiful words of Ann Ulanov, one who accompanies us on this journey of mediality, best describe my experience of the Holy:

> It is only religion, theology, the church's life that dares to go beyond this boundary-line of depth psychology, to brave the unknown waters, to cross beyond the known into the unknown. The psyche's life is crucial, is fundamental to anything and everything we do. It cannot be ignored or hopped over. Neither can it be or give us all. It leads us where we must go, into the soul's life and stops. We are deposited there at that core of audacity and suppleness, that yearning and daring for what is beyond, while we are still in the flesh of the here and the now. The soul now dares to speak of this other in its own life so different from our life. . . . The difference of emphasis is enormous. The soul's life, after all, has to do with joy, the joyous shock of difference, the difference of the Other who

comes through, who calls out, who pushes, punches, pounds, and addresses us, saying, "Here is what I have for you. Take it."[50]

The medial woman's special task is to listen to the calling, pushing, punching, pounding, and addressing of the soul and to communicate this with those who do not have the ears to hear it. In this light, the task of the medial is religious.

GUIDES INTO THE DEPTH

Each medial woman has and needs a guide or guides into the unconscious and unknown realms. Some of us have animal guides. For the medial women I've introduced you to earlier, Elizabeth is drawn forward by Bear, and Clelia has a close relationship with Penguin. Angela and Kathryn have angel guides. Turtle, Snake, and Owl accompany me.

Kathryn spoke of her angel guides. "Although I always keep my focus on God, I also feel that there are beings who are facilitating this. I've had lots of explanations as to who they are, and I've been given some names. *Nelnora* signs my pictures. My master teacher identifies himself as *Roblandro*, and I have a strong sense that he is a 'he.' I've had a vision of him, and he told me he was assigned to be my master teacher. There are beings other than Jesus who are of that same Christ-consciousness. These beings, who are allowed to communicate with me, are exclusively of that consciousness. In my training, I learned to work with angels. I feel I work with more than one angel, but my real desire is to work with Jesus."

Clelia said she loves penguins and feels more drawn to them than any other animal after a trip to Antarctica. "How like a penguin I am," she commented. "Penguins are short and tubby. They walk with a waddle, awkward and lacking grace on the land. *However*, when they are in the water, they are magnificent, and incredibly supple, appearing to be in a ballet. They are good family members and parents to their young, and they are generally faithful to their spouses. Of course, they like to live in communal settings, which I tried but found was not my thing. As for me, I've always seen myself as short, round, and awkward in movement, not graceful or athletic. However, in the unconscious, I have had repeated dreams of being incredibly graceful, dreams in which I am an ice skater skimming over the ice. And a dancer. Sometimes I float just above the ground in graceful movements. I can float down a stairway at great speed, never trip, fall, have to hold on or watch my feet. Although I have not dreamed specifically of penguins, in my dreams I am like the penguin gliding through the water. The penguin is a medial creature."

In writing about my own medial experiences, I must mention Turtle and Snake in some detail. Turtle lived in our home in the body of Blinky, our son Andrew's red-eared slider, whom we all loved, talked with, and tended, who moved away from home when Andrew did, and who will probably outlive us all. Turtle has appeared to me over many years in dreams, sometimes as Tortoise, sometimes as magnificent Sea Turtle, sometimes as little Blinky.

My connection to snakes comes from my daughter Alisa's many childhood pet snakes: Mr. Butterwick Callahan, Cortez, Sneaky, and Balboa. Though they were hers, they also became deeply connected to *my* soul. I'll never forget the night one of them died. She and a friend gently buried the snake in the garden. Through her many tears, I knew how deeply she loved these powerful, though small, creatures, which have, throughout time been symbols of healing, divine power (good or evil), feminine power, and the soul itself.

One of the most profound appearances of Turtle, which has shaped my life, is the following dream:

> I am standing with an old man, a guide, at the entrance to a cave. A young man standing with us points to the horizon, which outlines a city submerged in smog and smoke. He expresses his distress at the state of civilization and how we are rapidly destroying creation. I ask what city this is, but he doesn't answer, as though it could be any city. I feel frantic and want to do something to save the city. The guide then points to the cave, which has two entrances and is almost hidden with trees. At the edge of one entrance is a large, fluorescent pink tortoise. At the other are another tortoise and a huge snake. The guide calls the animals to him, and they move very close, the snakes wrapping themselves around his body, the turtles staying at his feet. I am afraid. Then the old man tells me to be still, neither to step on them nor disturb them, but simply *to be* in their presence.

This dream continues to be alive and to inform me years later. Rather than analyze it, I will share the context into which it came and why it has been so important.

I've already mentioned that from childhood, I've always felt that my purpose in life was to serve others, to meet their needs, to fix what is broken, and to bring hope, love, or peace. I have done this long and well, and ministry is certainly a profession that capitalizes on this tendency. Over the years, no matter what work I'm engaged in, I do it with full-heartedness, a sense of service, and commitment, whether it be cleaning closets, filing x-rays in a college summer job, raising kids, or leading a memorial service. Knowing my adaptability and tendency for excellence, I realize how significant it is for me to choose *where* to invest myself. I don't need to be the world's best x-ray file clerk. I've always known that I could be good at many tasks, but I need to be reminded that just because I am doing something, or something needs to be done, or I can do it well, it is not necessarily my call.

In college, when my primary work was studying, I still thought humble service was what I was called to do with my life. My parents were not particularly pleased when I went to Mississippi for a work project during spring vacation from college in 1964. And they put their feet down completely on my hopes to go back and register voters that summer. So, I had a lonely summer taking typing and accounting classes at a business college. Three men were killed as they registered voters that summer in Mississippi, so my folks were right. They were protecting me, but business classes were definitely not my call. That was years ago, and I've done my share of typing and accounting as well as service to humanity since then.

Suddenly and surprisingly in this dream, the old man points out that service to humanity or saving humanity was no longer the focus of my call. My vocation now was to be ever more fully in the presence of Turtle and Snake as they moved in and out of the dark cave of the unconscious underneath the burning city. For now, I must *be*, rather than *do*; for now, I must be *beneath*, rather than *above*; for now, I must say *"no"* to the obvious so that I can say *"yes"* to the hidden. There could not be a more difficult shift than the one that this dream was asking of me, nor could there be a more life-giving, energizing, powerful movement of soul than this.

Turtle speaks most eloquently of my experience of descent and resurfacing, of bridging these two realms, for Turtle is a creature of the land and water, of the surface and the depths. Turtle visits me in dreams which speak to the needs of my soul at the moment. When Turtle dries up, I need to allow my soul to dive beneath and be in the depth's dark, watery landscape. Able to remain underwater at a great distance for long periods, Turtle still must come to the surface for air. When accidentally caught in fishing nets and dragged along the bottom with no access to air, Turtle drowns. When Turtle drowns, *I* need to come up for air, to breathe the lively spirit again before returning to the depths. The dark watery soul needs the bright, airy spirit, if ever so briefly. Turtle moves to the rhythm of above and below, of dry and wet, of light and darkness. This is why the old man in the dream told me to "be with the Turtles."

Turtle also speaks of deep inner knowing. Traveling thousands of miles, Turtle comes to lay her eggs on the shore, the same shore upon which *she* hatched, and then she returns to her deep watery swim. She seems to know this by a sense within her body, not by having been carefully taught, not by trying and making mistakes, not by surveying the terrain and making clear decisions, but by a deep inner knowing. This is why the old man told me to "be with Turtle."

And what of Snake? Snake met me in another dream as a silver creature snuggled in my nearby slipper. At first, I was terrified, but as I engaged Snake in active imagination, Snake came near me, close and closer. Snake spoke these words to me:

> **Silver Snake:** I am the unexpected being. You were startled to see me: your feet were on the ground, and I was in your shoe. I come from the ground beneath your sole, holy ground upon which you stand barefoot. I've been waiting with you, waiting. . . beneath. My silver catches the night light. I am Snake of the night. I am Snake of the moon. I am Snake of the feminine. I wrap. I coil. I am the soft circle inside the shoe. I wait. I surprise. I am always with you but not always seen.

> **Golden Snake:** You glance away, and I am transformed. Now I am Golden Snake of the sun. I am not to be contained. I am swift, long, straight, and bright. I am the masculine. No longer round, my head is a diamond shape: four points each to be reckoned with. I move toward you because I need you to receive me. I need you to know that though I am removed from

you, I am part of you. I need you to claim me as your energy. I need to entwine myself around your body, to mix my venom with your blood. I am not satisfied with waiting any longer. I am part of you, and I will chase you until you embrace me. Why are you afraid?"

RC: I am terrified because I don't know you. I am afraid because you are fast and straight. I am afraid because you startled me. I am afraid because you are Other; you will poison me; you will kill me; you will make me other.

Days later, as I ventured back into this dialogue, and with trembling and open arms, I extended this invitation to Snake:

Slipper Snuggled Silver Snake
    I invite you to break free
                 to play
                 to move
                 to connect
                 to ascend.

    I invite you to span the paradox of both and neither
    I invite you to reveal yourself in the ascent
    I invite your appetite that swallows the whole
    I invite your stealth that surprises
    I invite your searching, sensitive tongue to discover the way
    I invite your supple strength
    I invite your adaptive thermostat
    I invite your ancient amphibiousness
    I invite your eyes which never close

Golden Snake
    I invite your essence into mine.

At these words, Golden Snake stopped chasing me, wrapped his form up the length of my body, and then encircling me, bolted in descent to become my Golden Backbone.

Surely, we human beings have within us that same inner knowing and essence as these creatures of the deep unconscious, but we have layered this over with so much refinement that it is lost and forgotten deep inside. Whether this wisdom is within our bodies or our psyches, I do not pretend to know; however, I envision that all realms of our being contain wisdom beyond imagining, which is there to be called upon. I also believe that our medial selves must become as basic, simple, and nonrational as Turtle and Snake to connect with this wisdom. This is why the old man in the dream told me to "be with the Turtles and the Snakes."

I stayed with the Turtle and Snake, and they have visited and guided me many times over the years. I'll share another dream of Turtle and Snake:

> I am in a class with people who are *my* people. My self-appointed job is watching and tending the turtles and snakes who are on the floor. We are rehearsing for a play. I can't remember my lines, but I am aware that the turtles and snakes are in danger of being stepped on, and I protect them. I feed them. One of the snakes is hurt, perhaps has been stepped on, and becomes two snakes. One of these snakes has an enlarged head and short body.
>
> I gather up the snakes and turtles and put them all in a tank while we leave for a while. I have difficulty keeping up with my classmates, so I return. When I return, I look at the animals and discover that one of the snakes has died. The others are healthy, so I feed them and watch them eat. This is my work.

Someone needs to tend the animals:
    low to earth
        open-eyed
            skin-shedding
                head-hiding
                    animals.

Animals
    who contain Truth
        which classes
            clinicians

thoughts
    theories
        erudition
            and logos
                can never capture.

Animals
who hold Wisdom of Earth:
    primitive
        first order
            close to chaos
                newly created
                    fully formed
                        Life.
Animals
Oblivious:
        to format
        to formation
        to information
        to transformation
                Underbelly of creation.

Animals
    Feasting on
        raw, primal life
  of sea
      waters
        depths
          now
            formed anew
              into scale
                into shell.

O Snake, O Turtle,
  Are you the cry of my soul
      without words?

Are you the pain that wells deep within

and departs untended?

Are you the quiet moment?
            the simple need?
                  the unself-conscious action?

Are you the wisdom before training?
            the longing before control?

O Turtle, O Snake:
    Are you the I
        who belongs to the earth?
        who claims the world as home?

Are you the balance
    between protection and vulnerability?
        between speed and caution?
            between stealth and strength?
                between land and water?

Are you what *the civilized* fear and ignore:
                as the world rushes,
                    as cities suckle smoke.

O Snake, O Turtle
            I trust that in time
                I will learn your secrets
                    of early, enduring creation.

Yet:
    for now,
            it is enough
                to be out of step:
                    tending,
                        attending,
                            being
                                with You.

This is why the old man told me simply to "be in the presence of the Turtles and the Snakes." Turtle and Snake, may we remember to be in your presence.

ENCOUNTERS AT THE LIMEN

All of the women to whom I've introduced you have spoken of a deep sense of their relationship with The Other. This Other may be called *God, The Collective Unconscious, The Holy, Hope,* or a myriad of different names, for it is difficult to know what to name this sense of Beyond, or even if it can be named. I've always respected the ancient Hebrew word for God, which is a transliteration of the symbols YHWH, meaning "I Am Who I Am," for this Holy Being is truly unnamable. And to some Jews, it is not to be spoken.

Although they are much alike, each medial woman I interviewed has had a different way and experience of mediating that which is beyond the earthly human realm. So, I invite us to return to their experiences.

Clelia experiences herself as a conduit for information coming from another realm, that of "Transpersonal Being." Being face to face with a Transpersonal Presence is a profound experience for her, even though it is difficult for her to name. As she channels this information, she has a sense that there is some kind of energy or being beyond her. She began to use the word *guide* as a description for that with whom she is in touch.

Kathryn receives information from beings she knows as angels who communicate their names directly with her. In fact, she told me that I even have a guardian angel named "Mabel." She feels privileged to know some of their identities. The angels who communicate with her do so physically through word, writing, drawing, picture, and movement. Kathryn identifies distinctions between God, Christ, and Angels.

Elizabeth is driven in her writing by a vital energy, which sometimes she personifies into voices or glimpses of visions. She experiences her writing as a partnership between the energy from Beyond and her own energy. Occasionally she has experienced something Absolutely

Other taking over and writing words that seemed not to be her own words.

Angela, as a child, had a strong sense of angels guarding her, angels which she could figuratively see. She had a personal relationship with Jesus and an assurance of God. Though her childhood conceptions have changed, she still has a deep connection with God and a deep knowing of Spiritual Reality.

I also have always had a deep sense of the presence of God and have experienced a connection not only with Jesus but also with those beyond death. As I've already mentioned, animals come from a deep place in the unconscious and are also present to me as guides and guardians. I experience a deep knowing, similar to Turtle's knowing in the midst of a journey of thousands of miles where and when to come to the shore to lay her eggs. The presence of angels in the courtroom gave me courage and perspective in one of life's most difficult experiences. I try to be open to whatever wants to come through and be known.

Most of what these women mediate comes from what Jung called the *collective unconscious*, a realm "detached from anything personal and . . . common to all, . . . since its contents can be found everywhere."[51] However, some of what is mediated comes as visions from the *personal unconscious*. Clelia could see and guide a friend to her stolen jewelry that the robbers had thrown into a hedge, though Clelia was nowhere nearby. Kathryn was called in by a search and rescue team and could envision a plane's wreckage in a remote region.

All of us experience a personal and relational quality in this realm of Beyond. All have had the experience of being outside space and time, which are qualities of the collective unconscious. All have experienced the "voice within," coming from the unconscious and pervading all our lives.[52]

Each woman is in touch with the realm of deepest longing, be it for healing, for the planet's future, for the expression of inner truth and wisdom, for connection with those who are gone, or for relationship with the divine. Linda Leonard reminded us that these women are all visionaries, "looking inward and listening in the dark temple of the earth to the deep silence, . . . [traveling] between the 'worlds' and [mediating] the messages from the spirit to the community."[53] We mediate both the small and the large, the "ah ha" and the "never to be understood." All of us have had experiences of mediating the realm of sacred space, that which is "everything beyond our intention, understanding, and control, the mysterious, the irrational, the realm beyond thing, thought, and word."[54] As we move back and forth between this world and the other, or as we stand at the entrance and mediate from this realm beyond, we are *liminal personae*. As such, we awaken and maintain a sense of awe and gratitude in relation to the unnamable realm which we mediate.

Like Clelia's penguins, when swimming in our water, we all move easily, fluidly, naturally, and regularly with the medial's archetypal tasks, if given the time, space, and solitude we need. Each of us longs to bring what she knows and experiences to the surface and to have a forum to share it for the common good. This can be a difficult task for all of us because we see and know what others may miss and find difficult to accept. Although medial women may accomplish much in the outer world, accomplishment is not the medial's primary task as she expresses what she knows.[55] Our native language is imagery and symbol; however, as we relate to the outer world, which uses many other languages, we must become multilingual to mediate what is beyond. Again, as Ann Ulanov has said, medial women listen to the "Other who comes through, who calls out, who pushes, punches, pounds, and addresses us, saying 'Here is what I have for you. Take it.'"[56]

THE LANGUAGE OF DREAMS

Medial women have diverse ways of knowing and communicating. For example, Kathryn and the angels communicate. Clelia and Kathryn are clairvoyant and can sometimes see what is not seen, even when they're not physically present. Elizabeth finds poetic words and images welling up within. Angela speaks the language of ritual and empathy. Most of us find dreams that come from the collective unconscious to be powerful ways of knowing.

Dreams are a profound experience for Clelia. She said, "Dreams have always been a connection to the other world for me. I don't have dreams all the time. There are special ones that pop in here and there, like gifts. Some cultures call them 'big dreams.' I've had dreams of being dead and still being able to interact with people in this realm. One dream I had a few years ago comes back to mind:

> I am with another woman, and we are walking along a path in a rural area where there aren't houses. We are laughing and having a good time, walking along feeling very good. Then we see some people who are struggling with a project. They want to raise money to help people sick with liver disease. It is a noble cause, so we stop and ask if we can help. They look at us strangely, and we back off. We say to each other, "Oh, my God, we know we look different, but maybe we better look into a mirror and see what they're seeing." So, we look into a mirror and see that we look tall, skinny, grayish, and sort of El Greco-ish. We look definitely different. And we say, "Oh dear, it's too bad. That's what's scaring them." So, we say to them, "Look, we know we look different. It's because we are dead, but that doesn't make any difference. We're really happy, and we can help you. So don't worry

about the fact that we're not alive." And we feel wonderful. We are just feeling so good that we can help them.

Clelia reflected on this dream. "It was just our appearance that was getting in the way, and the fact that we were dead didn't bother us at all. There is something different and special when you are between worlds, and you can help. There is a freedom. And we just felt very good about it. I've had dreams of people after their deaths, like my mother and my father, who just sort of reappeared, but I couldn't say that these were experiences of crossing into the realm of death."

Clelia continued, "My dreams seem to disappear when I get all this linear stuff going. It's like waking up and saying, 'Oh yeah, there's been a dream.' When I'm so caught up in all the rest, the dreams seem to stop. I have to have the time for the dreams to come again. My dreams seem to come out of the quietness of my soul or sometimes out of an evocative reading. They come back again, they sort of pick back up, as though they are saying, 'Oh, you're listening again, so here, I'll come back.' I need to listen."

Dreams are the most profound connection with the unconscious for me. In fact, I often mix up the words "dream" and "prayer." They both come from the same core place in my soul.

I have been blessed with strong dreams during much of my life, especially in times of need. Unfortunately, like Clelia, dreams seem to disappear when my life is steeped with the pressures of the outer, linear world. However, I know what actually has disappeared is my ability to receive them openly.

My dreaming did not meet with much enthusiasm from my mother, who confessed that she "never dreamed," though in her later life, she too had a dream that revealed the secret of the death of her best friend who had disappeared on a hike, never to be found again. It may have made a difference in her response to my dreaming if her *one* dream had come earlier, but it didn't. I remember feeling devastated once as a child when I told her a dream and she responded that she thought I was making it up. Many times, she cooled my sharing of dreams by saying that it was bad luck to tell dreams before breakfast. I learned not to speak of my dreams. This may be why I so often asked myself, "Is there a place for me?"

Years ago, my analyst listened to my dreams and heard them call me into deeper work. I had come for consultation because I felt

devastated by not being able to find a graduate school of psychology
that honored both psyche and spirit. I thought these concerns could
be handled in three therapeutic sessions, during which he would help
me find the right school. However, I ventured to share with him
dreams of falling, dreams of crashing, and a dream of a baby ready to
be born and having to punch its little fist through my abdomen to
attract my attention. These attracted *his* attention. He suggested I
work for a while in therapy on my soul before I considered finding a
school. Over many years, I worked intensely with dreams, shown the
way by this sensitive, soulful person. Together, the dreams and the
analyst have guided and guarded me, drawn me into dark places and
brought me back, shown me what I would rather not look at, and
revealed mystery beyond imagining. Actually, I finally did find my
school, Pacifica Graduate Institute, a school which was not even in
existence when I began the analytic process, a school whose motto is
Animae Mundi Colendae Gratia: "For the Sake of Tending Soul In and
Of the World."

Dreams are honored at my graduate school of depth psychology.
For example, the assignment in one course was to amplify a dream
and share it in class. The dream I worked with was simple: Turtle was
drowning, and his shell was swelling and coming off in pieces. I had
ventured to amplify this watery dream with a progression of watercol-
ors and lay the sheets of paper down on the floor with the class
gathered around as I explained the landscape of water, the death of
this creature, and how I had carried it forward in the paintings. Suddenly my angst came forth, and deep tears from the core of my being
arose, as my astonished classmates drew closer to me on the floor,
and the teacher, Pacifica's founder, Dr. Stephen Aizenstat, led me
deeper through the dreamscape to a protective place of grounding.

The next day Dr. Aizenstat talked privately to each of us who had
shared a dream in the class. I was astonished by what he said to me
and wrote it down so that I would remember.

> Cultures around the world would navigate to this dream. It is
> a shamanic dream, a big dream. They would build tradition
> around it for generations to come, and it would assume a cen-
> tral place in the community context. Your task is to witness
> the vision. You are a porous person. For you, the boundaries
> between life and death are permeable, and you are a guide for

people back and forth between this world and the other realm. This is surely what you do in your ministry, why you are sought after, but you must let go of the bureaucracy and pay attention to tending and witnessing the vision. It is time for you to move beyond the personal and into the realm of the archetypal, the world soul.[57]

This response was a far cry from being told that I have made up my dreams. I cannot remember what it was in sharing this dream that brought such profuse tears. Perhaps I was mourning the death of my medial soul, which Turtle had come to represent. Yet I will never forget the experience of having this dream, sharing it, and having two dozen classmates surrounding me on the floor, almost as though they became my shell, my home. Not only was the dream honored, but so was I, the dreamer.

Many people claim *not* to have dreams, even medial women; however, we all have dreams, most of which aren't tended. Tending dreams takes intention and effort, as they can easily slip back into unconsciousness. For me, dreams have been my guide into the depths to which I pay attention.

PROFOUND LONGINGS

I believe that every human being has a longing for the spiritual, which has been expressed in so many ways throughout time and place. One of my greatest privileges as a minister and a therapist has been to witness and accompany people on their quests. Of course, we are time-bound and culture-bound when it comes to our understanding of the great Mysteries, and humility is necessary as we search. Medial women have a slightly different and perhaps more urgent longing for a refined relationship with the spiritual than many others. And so now, I turn to explore this.

Hungering for Quietness

My research showed that medial women need an inordinate amount of quietness, and if we are given this, we can find solace within.

Sometimes, Angela shared, she would simply close her office door to find this. Other times she went to the beach or mountains alone. In these times, she was best able to hear God's voice and be replenished. She knew she was not called to stay near the waves forever, tempting though it might seem. Rather, this quietness of nature allowed her to go back into the world to do what she must do. In her aloneness, even if it was just reading romances alone in the bathroom in the middle of the night, Angela discovered that she was often able to leave her daily self and "become other."

Clelia stated "I am fanatic about needing my own space and my own quiet time. One of the reasons I love living where I do is that it is very quiet. When I wake up in the morning, I hear the birds and the ocean, not traffic. Not everyone understands this huge need for quietness. When I'm constantly in the extroverted world, all I get is the noise. I feel I have to be quiet just to process everything I have picked up. In the quietness, things come together as they need to, but not from here to there in a straight line. Often, I'm so burdened with the linear duties, which I'm good at, that I don't leave enough time for my spiritual self. Then I remind myself of Thich Nhất Hanh finding great joy in each moment or task, and I say to myself, 'Wait a minute; don't try to blow up. He has found this beauty and this joy just step, by step, by step, each day. He doesn't seem to feel trapped.'

"This need for quiet is to allow the connection between the realms. When I'm very busy with scheduled things, to-do lists to follow, meetings to go to, and just running around, it feels like the medial part of me gets shut off because all this other is taking the space. It's only in the quiet times that I find myself again, even if I'm busy doing something which doesn't take mental concentration but is more mechanical. I can be cooking, clipping flowers, dead-heading stuff in the garden, something like that where my mind can just drift. It's not in the place of *no thought*. It's more like drifting. Amazing things pop up in that time because it's not a linear thing I'm doing. I'm just letting my mind drift. And it's then when insights, thoughts, or feelings come up."

Clelia continued, "It's very hard to create quiet space and still be part of the world; in fact, it's a constant battle for me. I'll find some space, maybe even make a new way to create it, and that goes okay for a little while, and then it gets used up again. I have fantasies of giving it all up and going and living in a monastery forever, fantasies I've had since childhood. I was going to be a nun. So, I've had this pull, but I chose not to become a nun. I do choose to be in the world, to be married, but there's still this pull to the quiet, enclosed place."

Elizabeth's childhood family knew her need for alone time and silence and gave this to her in her own room. She told me that her soul *must* have quiet time and space, which she uses for daydreaming and writing; given quiet time and inner space, she has all she needs within herself. If she doesn't have this time and space, she admits to being no good on the worldly level. She learned to tune out her chatty neighbor as they walked together, and was able to find a bit of solitude as she got some exercise.

Kathryn found that the world's needs were using her up, so she began to work with daily meditation. In doing this, she experienced a renewal of energy, and in this practice, she began to discover her unique gifts for healing. She continued the practice of meditation in order to keep herself clear as a channel.

I have always thrived on silence and times of aloneness. As a child, the deep silence of forests or the crashing of waves on the coast gave me a sense of who I was and where I belonged. Later, amid our busy ministry and being a mom, I held Mondays when the kids were in school to be alone and do laundry, housecleaning, and grocery shopping. My soul could move into reflection and prayer while my body did the necessary, mindless tasks. During this time of my life, I took short silent retreats and discovered that the prayers I wrote there became poetry of a sort. I had never written poetry before, and though I had majored in English, I had never even taken a creative writing course because I doubted I was creative. Yet, I found a creative inner voice in the stillness.

Whether silence is found simply by being in a quiet place or through intentional meditation, I have discovered that when I am there, the fragments of my life come together in new ways and that creativity wells up and again begs for expression.

My deepest prayer arises out of silence, a time of uncluttering my soul and opening to the holy within and beyond, to the people and issues of concern, and to the places of intense gratitude. I find it essential to have regular periods of silence, which may be as simple as a day of housecleaning without answering the telephone, an afternoon retreat, a long drive in which my husband and I share solitude together, or a gentle nap. Retirement has given me more of the gift of silence than I've ever had before. It is a season of life that has brought unexpected and wonderful surprises.

Medial women require more silence than most people to keep their souls alive and fresh. Quietness is necessary for each of us and is a significant loss for us when it is not available, which in our culture is *usually*.

Yearning in Childhood for the Spiritual

As medial women, my research participants and I all chose to go to church as young children, and four of us actually went alone. Growing up as a child in my culture, the church seemed to be the primary way to find a connection with the holy. Each of us longed deeply for this.

Clelia's family was nominally Catholic but did not attend Mass. Clelia chose to go to the church on her own, went to catechism, was confirmed, struggled with the church's doctrine, and continued to attend Mass by herself until she was a young adult.

Kathryn's parents did not attend church. Her father was philosophical but not religious, and her mother was deaf and could not understand the service. However, Kathryn was drawn to attend worship as a child and went to various Protestant churches on her own.

Angela's mother did not go to church after she had been deeply hurt there, but Angela wanted to be in church. Her grandparents supported her going to church, and when they didn't go together to the Methodist church, they allowed her to walk down the street alone to the Baptist church.

She reflected on her childhood spirituality this way: "This deep sense of knowing began when I was a child and has been a large part of who I have been all my life. When I was a young child, there were pictures that for me were absolutely real, such as a picture of an angel with two little children walking across a bridge. I had no doubt that the two children were my brother and me. That angels were mounted in the corners of my room was not even a question for me. I could see them; it was not a matter of their having solid form, but I could see them spiritually. As a child, Jesus was a friend. He was not a name or an image; rather, I simply knew he knew who I was. This deep knowing began as an assurance of knowing God and the Spirit intimately as a little person, having consciousness of this presence, having a great desire to be in church, and being transported by the music. As a child, I vacillated between wanting to be a nun, though I wasn't Catholic, and a social worker when I grew up. There was the sense of both of them holding and helping people."

Elizabeth went to the United Church of Christ with her family throughout her childhood, and after college, she even began seminary as she considered ministry as her profession. She is the only one of these women whose family accompanied her to church as a child. She recounts an early experience that "could be part of my medial longing for a deep connection with the holy, though I wouldn't have known what to call it at the time. This took place at a small chapel where my family went for my uncle's wedding, when I must have been three or four; it is one of my earliest memories. Though I had no concept of the holy, no expectation of churches or chapels, I do remember this as a *very desirable place*. I'm sure it must have been spiritual to me. The light in there was special. The wood was so warm feeling, and there was a small pipe organ that we walked by, and I wanted to hear music on it. The whole time I just really wanted to be in that space and explore. However, I wasn't allowed to do that because we had to sit down, be contained, behave, and witness the wedding. That place always seemed magical to me. Years later, I returned there; I had the same feeling. When I think of places I would want to go and just be by myself and try to open to my spirituality, this one's high, high on the list."

Though my own family had no church affiliation, I wanted to attend church as a three-year-old, and my parents obliged me by dropping me off for Sunday School and then picking me up. I'll never forget coloring the outlined stained-glass windows on a mimeographed paper I brought home from Sunday School with the 23rd Psalm written on it. It was a rainy Sunday afternoon, and I hunkered down on my bed with all my many colors of crayons to create something beautiful. I was just learning to read, so I loved the words, the shapes, and the colors. I loved the church. When I came home one day and asked why I was "the only Christian in the family," my parents said that they looked at each other and began to come with me to church, but it was years later when they actually joined and participated. I preferred to attend worship rather than go to Sunday School as a child, which may have been because worship was an *experience of* the holy instead of a *conversation about* it. Over the years, I participated in both, but I always preferred worship with the music, the scripture, the prayers, the words, the high ceilings with a little bit of gold painted into the wood, and what I felt was the clear presence of God. I loved the beauty of it all, and later I learned that the word for "beauty" in the Navajo language is the same as the word for "God." I longed to be in the presence of the holy, even as a small child.

As an early woman in United Methodist ministry, I had to struggle against being slotted into the roles of Christian educator or Youth Group counselor, where women in those days were expected to serve the church. I was never comfortable there; I was called to be a minister, to lead worship and guide people spiritually. That would not be such a problem now, more than 50 years later, as there are more women than men in seminary and all levels of ministry, and it is no longer the assumption that women are only to be educators.

I have found nothing in my review of the literature written about the medial child's early religious experiences and desire to connect with the holy. It is significant that each of these medial children wanted to be in church and that four of the five of us wanted to be there so much that we went alone as little girls.

Questing for the Beyond and Beneath Throughout Life

My research participants and I are medial women on a spiritual quest, which keeps opening before us the farther we journey.

In the early part of my visits with Angela, she stated that she had been drawn into the holy and away from the imbalance of worldly life. As a child, she always had a sense of God's presence in her life, but this was interrupted when she was nine, around the time sexual abuse began. She said she was not in touch with God again until she was 42, though she continued on an inward journey during the interim. "My rage was large, and when you're raging that hard, you can't hear God's voice within you; you lose yourself." She had been a part of various churches but did not always find grace there.

Clelia's spiritual quest took her from the Roman Catholic Church to Jehovah's Witnesses, which did not fit her, to Transpersonal Psychology, to the realms of Buddhism and Hinduism, and then even back into a Roman Catholic Church. Clelia did not tie her spirituality into any particular form of expression now but continued working with it in deeper, broader ways. She thrived on an open discussion of matters of the soul and spirit. She had a vivid dream some years ago, which she recounted in this way:

> "In it was a figure or a being, whom I couldn't see but could feel. He said, 'I'd like to take you on a tour and show you some very important things.' We rose above earth, floating in the heavens. Then he said, 'I want you to look down on earth.' I could see these sorts of rectangles, and there were little lights, like little, teeny Christmas lights, and he said, 'Now each one of these rectangles you're seeing represents a person's life, and each light marks love given or received. Nothing else matters, such as being rich or poor, type of job or education. What matters is love received and love given.'"

She shared this dream with a continuing sense of awe. For her, this was the Transpersonal Being, a conduit for information coming from another realm, which she said may be what is called *the unconscious*. While she was "not sure where this stuff comes from," she did know that it traveled with her, or she with it. This was a profound experience that she has tried to hold and keep.

Elizabeth continued to keep her connection with the church of her childhood. She also discovered that her spirit needed a big space within herself and experienced a deepening and widening within, as though there she found an inner chapel, a sanctuary, or a cathedral where she met the holy. She engaged the questions along her spiritual journey with intellectual as well as feeling energy and enjoyed the questions as a part of the quest.

Kathryn's spiritual journey took her from a rather ordinary relationship with a church to the systematic development of her personal gifts of healing, which were not understood within the mainline church. This led her to participate and then be ordained in a church that stood in the New Age tradition, which was not entirely comfortable for her. Finally, she found a mainline Protestant Church whose pastor could accept what she chose to share of her gifts. Her spiritual journey was not bound by the church, but rather the church was a community that she needed and a place where her gifts could be contained, albeit largely undercover.

Kathryn continued to be open to whatever direction she was being called to move and grow. She shared: "It is important for anyone who tries to understand who I am to have an understanding of the way I experience the universe. Much of creation is unseen and mysterious, though some of this can be known. I call the source of revelation *God* because I tend to be a simple person. I just work with God and ask to be his channel. I have much reason to have faith because in being used in this way, I've come to know that whoever or whatever is working through me is All Knowing and All Loving. Since I'm called upon every day of my life, I can see the order and the goodness of life, and I know I can trust that what I need will be given. I never take my eyes off God, the number one rule. If I keep this focus, I will be protected and given what I need in every situation. I have sought nothing and have been given everything."

I have always chosen to be open to the mystical experiences that have come to me throughout my life, usually when I least expect them.

Part of my journey is not only to experience these but also to name them. The church has been a setting where these experiences can be held, but they are not contained by the church or limited to the church, and the demands of ministry can even close them down. I appreciate the distinction between soul and spirit, with soul embracing that which is deep, dark, moist, and feminine, and spirit reaching upward to the airy, bright, and transcendent. Holding both is necessary for my personal journey.

I remember occasional afternoons as a child going to the Stanford campus with my father. After visiting his parents, he would take us to play on the hilly grass of The Circle Drive, and then we would go with him into the Stanford Chapel. The chapel is lined with windows of deep primary-colored stained glass, portraying images of Biblical stories, and high above these hover angels of gold and pastel mosaic tile. Words could not describe what I experienced every time I went into that chapel. I knew that someday I would know those stories in the windows, and I was convinced that those angels already knew me, a little girl in a big space.

As a pre-teen, I remember at least two times when I could feel the presence of Jesus and knew without a doubt that I would always love him. One of these times occurred while I was reading Lloyd Douglas's book *The Robe*, which I found on my grandfather's shelf. The other time happened while I was reading a book for my Sunday School class, of all places. I always felt that Sunday School books were dry, boring, and somewhat demeaning, but this one seemed to be intended for adults rather than sixth graders; it was different because it spoke of Jesus in ways more powerful than childish. In both experiences, I had difficulty breaking away from the mystical encounter and going back into the family activities. I have always had a hard time leaving the experiences of the holy.

Throughout my teen years, I continued to be drawn to spiritual areas. In junior high, I wrote a book review of *A Man Called Peter*, and recall being moved by the sermons, prayers, and biography of Peter Marshall, who had been the chaplain to the Senate. For a tenth-grade English assignment where we were to write a dialogue, I created a conversation between Abraham of Ur, Joan of Arc, and Billy Graham, three faithful figures across traditions, millennia, and miles. I still have that paper in which Billy Graham entertains Abraham and Joan in his home and introduces them to black-and-white television.

As I moved through high school, I was always glad to assume the leadership for the faith aspects of our youth groups, to help lead high school youth group retreats, and to participate in worship leadership for the whole church. Interestingly, I never had to compete for leadership positions in this area. I guess most teens were more interested in the action and fellowship parts of the youth group. I was one of the few who would be up early for Morning-Watch on retreats because those quiet moments alone in the woods filled my soul. They are moments that I will always remember.

Thomas Moore described experiences of deep centering like I had as "everything beyond our intention, understanding and control. It is that which is big and holds a quality of attraction and power. When we empty out our intention, the sacred is present. Holy things need space."[58]

I was disappointed with seminary, which was very academic and had little of the soulful or spiritual in it when I was there. Sadly, in my opinion, many denominations currently seem to be struggling with their spiritual health, reason for existence, and ideological splits. Amidst all the busyness in the churches I know, there is only occasionally something available within to feed my soul. Have mainline denominations become corporate? Have they lost their imagination? Have I changed? Has the language of faith changed? I also know that the chaos and uncertainty of change can be creative, so I hold hope for what is to emerge as Church.

Again, I call to mind the dream I shared earlier of the butterfly at the burning church, which was so hot that it lit a candle in the bag in which I carried it, but didn't burn the bag. I know there is a butterfly and a lit candle hidden from our vision but carried forward, which will bring a transformed church and a new language of faith into a new age.

I remind us of Ann Ulanov's words that psyche "leads us where we must go, into the soul's life and stops. We are deposited there at the core of audacity and suppleness, that yearning and daring for what is beyond, while we are still in the flesh of the here and the now. The soul now dares to speak of this other in its own life so different from our life."[59]

OUR GIFTS

When I wrote my dissertation, I had to narrow it down so much that I focused mainly on the *wounds* of medial women in our culture, which were dark experiences. But now that I can explore our natures more fully in my own way, I'm discovering many more qualities about us that are worth noting, which I think show up as the light side of the medial. I have discovered that our wounds are our gifts turned inside out; our gifts are our wounds turned inside out.

Angela, Clelia, Elizabeth, and Kathryn, my medial friends, as well as Toni Wolff and other wise poets, writers, and thinkers, are here to help us explore these. Here are some of our experiences of our many gifts.

Empathy

It is not unexpected that all the medial women I know have the quality of empathy: deep, spontaneous, natural, strong empathy. Empathy is a quality that seems to have been present from our earliest childhoods rather than having been trained into us. It is at the heart of our relationships, decisions, and interactions in the world, yet others may or may not understand the depth from which it comes.

Clelia's empathy connected her to what was happening with other people and could cause her deep pain when the hurts of the world came in too closely. She commented that she broke into tears when she was in Russia soon after the fall of the Soviet Union. "We went to one of the churches, and seeing the old women pitifully holding out their hands and begging, was almost too much. These old women were caught in the changes of the new regime, which just wiped them out. Although it can be so painful, even overwhelming, I think the medial quality allows me to go through to other women, to other people, and feel what they feel. It hurts."

Kathryn's empathy came out partly through her clairsentience, which allowed her to know what another feels, though they are not in the same physical proximity and may not even know each other. She shared: "Clairsentience can cause a lot of complications. For one thing, if people have ill feelings toward me, I tend to feel *their* feelings. I tend to accept *their* feelings toward me because I sense into them, and I don't really recognize at the time that this is what I'm doing. At the same time, someone who doesn't experience this sense would own their personal feelings and look at the situation more objectively. I tend to accept people's criticism of me because I actually feel what they're feeling. It is sometimes difficult to sort out the difference between my feelings and someone else's feelings."

Elizabeth reflected on how her body always carried others' feelings. She experienced that her body carried part of her mediality; this showed up early in childhood and has also been part of her wounding. She shared: "I have a tendency to take another person's feelings into my own body. Often this was in relationship with my mother. My earliest memory stems back to being up late when my father was out of town on research trips. I remember pacing back and forth across the pillows of my parents' bed, putting my hand on the headboard, and feeling the rough texture of the wall with my little fingers, harsh to a child's hand. I remember the texture of the wall, that feeling still in my body, but when I follow it a little way, it leads me to my mother's anxiety. She was always anxious when he was gone. I missed him, but on some level, I knew that my mother didn't feel comfortable or safe. I remember being sick every time he would leave, probably through my high school years. I think my body took upon itself my mother's strong feelings, even her depression."

I intuitively learned early in life to respond to my mother's and father's needs and then was trained by my mother to respond to *any* presenting needs even before they were spoken. I took my mother's feelings into my own being so completely as a child that my own well-being was linked to her well-being. I grew up unconsciously knowing that there was no room for my own unique feelings and responses, so I didn't express, or perhaps even feel, many of them. While the empathy that comes from merging is not healthy, I have used my gift of empathy in my work and my relationships, and it has become a strong part of my uniqueness.

Angela was known to those near her as having something "extra." People expressed gratitude to her for the quality of her presence, her listening, and her knowing them in deep places, which was part of her spirit as well as a deeper, holy spirit.

Relationships are important to medial women, even though Wolff said that the archetype is "impersonal." I have come to understand that *what* is mediated is impersonal, and *standing at the limen* is impersonal. Still, the relationship to the *recipient* of the content that is mediated can be highly personal.

All of the medial women I know are characterized by their empathy. Part of this unique and deep resonance originates in the particular porosity of the medial person's psyche, which is different from the kind of empathy that originates in the feeling function. Rather than merely feeling *with* another person, the empathy of the medial woman comes from the ability *to see into or through* another person's experience and feelings.

Broad-Mindedness

We medials also speak of ourselves as being eclectic, broad-minded, and desirous of embracing that which is different from ourselves.

Although Clelia was a Roman Catholic, as a child and youth, she struggled with that church's theology of exclusion and finally left it as a young adult. Since then, she studied and participated in many forms of religious expression and understood the variety of religions as "different forms that are appropriate to different people at different times in different countries." She sought the deeper spirit beneath institutions and found fulfillment in "esoteric expressions which connect everyone."

Following an experience of being rejected by the Presbyterian church because of their distrust and dislike of her mediality and spiritual gifts, Kathryn found a home in a "church which is open to people shunned by traditional religions." She was also respectful of people's inability to understand who she was and what she really did, so she was careful not to push them beyond their belief systems as she worked with them.

Elizabeth told me, "It has always been easy for me to understand different perspectives and points of view. Actually, it has been so easy that I have always had trouble making decisions. I can understand every side of an issue. Even studying literature in junior high or high school, I could just slide into different perspectives, different cultures, and different time frames." She mentioned that she didn't really rebel as a teen because she could always see, respect, and empathize with her parents' points of view, even if they were different from hers. One of her deep fears was the potential backlash to her writing by closed-minded, rigid people.

Angela was brought up in a home of openness to different perspectives. There were no clear "rights and wrongs," few judgments or restrictions, and she experienced no shame in expressing herself differently as a child. She described herself as "an inclusive person, in which depth is not a narrow hole. In fact, I am extremely bothered by the kind of narrowness that says, 'God will only come to you through *this* medium.' That is a violation of being. It's almost like not being able to breathe. It's robbing one of what it means to be alive. My favorite scriptural passage is Romans 14, which says there is room for the one who believes and for the one who doesn't. It is much easier for me to accept this than the traditions that lead people on tirades that say, 'Only *this* way is okay, and all of the other people will be left out.' I want an amazon to go in there and work the shreds out of them. I can't do it, so I remove myself and stay away, but I just go bananas when they split everyone into us/them categories."

I have served congregations with people of many nationalities, ethnic groups, ages, as well as differing abilities and have had the privilege of knowing diverse people in intimate ways. I do not hold my perspective on faith as the highest or only one, and I struggle with people of faith traditions that do. In fact, much of my faith continues to grow. Though I was raised in an environment where morality was often presented in black-and-white terms, I have always been aware of shades of gray. As an adult, I have learned not only to move through the many hues of gray but also to see the beauty of colors. In addition, I have learned to hold together the opposites that my parents tended to polarize. Working as a private practice therapist has opened up my perspective even more. Having heard many experiences of many diverse people, I find myself slow to judgment.

The experience, norms, and values of a family or culture tend to construct what is considered "reality," and whatever does not fit into *this* structure of *this* reality tends to be relegated to the edges. As one begins to honor and move into the collective unconscious, which is the container of all human experience and all life experience, one discovers that the norms and values of any given family or culture are simply too small to define reality. It is ironic that in her very broadmindedness, the medial woman can threaten the culture in which she lives, and she is relegated to the edges by its narrow-mindedness. This may be why she feels most at home on The Other Side or at least seeing The Other Side, where there are no edges.

Healing

Most of us, somewhere in our lifetimes, have had the experience when someone truly sees us and knows what we need. This often has a mysterious quality, and we may ask, "How did they know?"

One therapist I know told the story of a patient who commented that her inner child felt "frozen in the ground." The therapist responded, "Tell me about frozen." Together they went to that deep, cold place in her psyche and sat next to that part until it thawed, which took weeks.

This is an example of medial healing. Though we live in a scientific age of evidence-based healing techniques, throughout history there have been avenues of healing that are grounded in intuition and call upon realms other than those centered in data. I'll point to three unique paths of healing grounded in the medial.

Curanderas are healers found mainly in Latin America and Mexico. They practice folk medicine, blending herbs and natural sources, such as mud and water, with versions of Catholic prayer and images of saints. To those interested in folk healing, I commend the beautiful, well-researched historical novel written by Luis Alberto Urrea entitled *The Hummingbird's Daughter.* A masterful storyteller, Urrea is the great-nephew of Teresita, the daughter of a wealthy landowner and a poor Yaqui Indian mother known as Hummingbird, who is a healer. Teresita was born with a red triangle on her forehead, and immediately the midwife knew that Teresita would have great power, for she too had been born with that sign. Through her healing abilities and deep compassion, Teresita became known as Sainta Teresa, and because of her strength in calling for native resistance to the repressive government, she has been called Mexico's Joan of Arc.

Witches have been seen as the opposite of healers in many times and cultures, for they have been commonly known as those who practice sorcery and magic and cast evil spells to harm the community. Shadowing them around the globe and throughout history has been the experience of being hunted, tortured, and killed. Most who were known as witches were actually healers and were innocent women burned alive by the fear of "godly men."

One tender insight into a woman called *witch* is the historical novel *The Highland Witch* by Susan Fletcher. This is a story that brings tears. Set in Scotland, it is based on the events of the 1692 Glencoe Massacre and begins with the storyteller, Corrag, imprisoned in a dungeon awaiting her day to be burned at the already constructed stake. Corrag and her mother are both healers who use their knowledge of herbs and the forces of the natural world in their works of compassion. Whether Corrag is a historical figure or not is unknown, but this novel captures the innocence and the horror of so many medial women who have been accused of being evil and demonic. Depicted in this tale are the fear, hatred, and unspeakable brutality that medial women have experienced in blatant forms, which continue at a cellular and a physical level to haunt some today.

Psychotherapists are modern, trained, licensed healers. Some therapists are medial people; many are not. Nevertheless, I suspect most therapists could speak to moments in a session when something Other entered the room. Depth therapists, trained in listening to the unconscious as it appears, tend to experience many of these moments, which a diagnosis or evidence-based techniques can't define. As I have sat in my office observing and listening to a client in the other chair, often I've become aware that the space between us is filled with a force that is neither theirs nor mine. It is the presence of a Third, an energy that shows up unexpectedly, bringing insight, knowing, awe, connection, and healing. Such numinous moments are not easily defined, but the therapist and patient often recognize them.

Another therapist shared with me about a patient who dreamed of being lost in a dark storm in a forest and then saw a small cabin in the distance. She knew that this cabin was just for her. When the therapist asked her to draw the cabin between sessions, this patient actually *constructed* the cabin out of cherry twigs and pine cone fragments with a removable roof. She brought it in for the next session and brought it into every session for years. She puts small objects into that cabin representing what needs to be protected in her psyche and life. Contents of dreams became part of her cabin and they live their imaginal lives in relationship to it. The client gets the cabin out at home when she needs a place of safety during distressing or frightening times, which calms her down. The combined work of the therapist and the patient, along with welcoming the unforeseen movements of the unconscious, enabled the expansion of this single image and allowed it to move deeper and deeper over time. That is medial healing.

In my own practice, I once worked with an artist, a young, suffering person whose abstract art was filled with dark colors and jagged, angular shapes. Often at our sessions, we both sat on the floor, where he put what he had created during the week between us. We talked, but we also listened with the ears of our hearts to the images, shapes, and colors on the floor. That space, filled with the artistic outpouring of his pain, became the voice of his psyche.

As depth therapists, we are called to guide our patients to become aware of how the unconscious penetrates consciousness, perhaps through dreams, synchronicity, moments of awe, unexplained experiences, or bodily symptoms. Depth therapists recognize that within each person is a medial part that may respond to the healing that comes from the Other. Our work is to mediate the emerging archetypal images with the patient's conscious life, slowly and carefully. We identify the opposites that tug at a patient's psyche, which cause confusion and chaos. In doing so, we enable that person to hold them until there is resolution and growth—"individuation," Jung would call it.

Our work is slow. Our tools are the depth of our psyches, coupled with our training in listening to and naming the unconscious, as well as our deep, intuitive empathy. Opportunities for healing are often missed. I think of a patient I once had whose parents wanted her to be a doctor. She was floundering in medical school and failing courses because she wanted to be a psychologist, not a medical doctor. Her parents, who controlled her life, fired me as her therapist because I refused to try to make her "want to become a doctor." They did not allow us to move to her life's real issues and longings. Those who want quick fixes and manipulation do not understand the nature of our work. However, growth comes to those who are open to the energy that shows up in a deep relationship with a healer and a deep connection with the Other, be it the unconscious or another unnamed transcendent quality. This is a natural setting for the healing gift of the medial person today.

Truth-telling

We medial women are responsible for bringing forth universal truths no matter the nature of the content. These truths come directly from the unconscious through images, dreams, inner voices, words, ideas, or our bodies. We must trust what we know and act according to the call to mediate this. It can feel strange to have insights that others might not have. I've discovered that sometimes these visions or insights disappear as quickly as dreams and dive right back into the unconscious. It has become important to me to speak or to write them, to make note of them when they arise so that in some way, I might bring them into the material world when the time is right.

Most of these women also have shared the importance of truth, which is spacious and expansive for the medial woman rather than narrow and exclusive.

Kathryn based her life on her conviction of the truth that God worked through her. She experienced this as a simple, powerful truth that she trusted, and she said she never took her eyes off God.

Angela spoke of invoking part of herself to be present to the truth when she studied so that she could hear and sift it on a deeper level than the one that was presented. As an avid reader, Angela was constantly searching for deeper truths.

Elizabeth was most comfortable trusting poetic truth. "I'm very much a person who has to speak the truth. I can't stand falsity. In those situations when I am molding myself into the environment, I really tend to shut down. If I close off one part of myself, it takes a lot of energy; it wastes a lot of energy. I really need to be a truth-teller to be who I am." To be a truth-teller required sorting out her truth from that of others. In fact, she used a pseudonym as she wrote her truth because of her fear of what her truth could mean in the world.

I was raised in a home where truth began with a capital "T" and was a measurable, logical, once-and-for-always-given, supported by data. My mother told me I might as well tell the truth because she would *always* find it out if I hadn't. I believed her, and when I hedged or outright lied, she always did find out. "The Truth" was *her* truth, of course; in her definition, there was usually only *one* truth. No "alternative truths" existed at that time. I was not allowed to consider that there may be many levels of truth or different perspectives on truth. Truth was a raw diamond rather than one with many facets that shone differently in other lights. It was never worth my arguing a point because I could never convince my mother of my unique perspective, and I knew that I could end up causing a rift in our relationship. I also was never able to argue in her logical, rationalistic way, based on her accurate recall of numbers and facts, and I often felt foolish. Literal truth-telling is a quality I tried to develop, though sometimes it was hard because I didn't fully participate in the literal world. It has taken me a lifetime to find my inner truth and claim that it is really truth. Still, that inner truth is often too frightening to speak out for fear that it will be disregarded, hurtful to another, or that I will be discounted as naïve or odd.

Linda Leonard offered helpful wisdom to us about the uniqueness of a medial woman's truth-telling:

- The visionary's "destiny is to reveal the universal truths of existence that encompass not only the beautiful but also the terrible."[60]

- "To see and then forget is to leave oneself open to ambiguity and disparagement by skeptics because one is not giving expression to the mysteries."[61]

- The ultimate challenge for the visionary is "to accept responsibility for what she sees and to be able to give her visions embodied form, expressing them, no matter how strange and enigmatic they seem."[62]

To communicate her unique visions and truth requires the medial woman to have extraordinary courage and a base of unconditional support. These medial women have found encouragement in family or a therapist, friend, pastor, or teacher. To express the truths she knows, the medial woman must be bilingual, proficient in the languages of both mystery and the ordinary. All of us enjoy what Leonard calls "faith and trust that the cosmos is a 'spiral dance' and wants us to be there as revealers and revelers."[63] Yet, as medial women, all of us have struggled at one time or another to be who we are, to get our truth out, and to circle back from the fear of being disbelieved or injuring another.

Imagination

We medials tend to be women of fantasy and imagination. In this way, we choose to hold reality lightly and allow it to move into various shapes and forms.

Elizabeth's favorite childhood activity was imagining and participating in pretend roles, but she was also prone to daydreaming, allowing her imagination to bloom. As she told me of her tendency to daydream, she said: "It was simply not understood by my goal-oriented family. That's what I like to do. I like to daydream. At school, I could be who I needed to be and attend to everything with excellence. At home, when I could let down and be who I really was, the daydreaming was right there, but it was judged as lazy or procrastinating, especially by my rational father, who had trouble understanding anything emotional or just nonproductive. What was wrong with me? Well, nothing was wrong with me. Daydreaming is just a part of who I am, and yet I always thought it was bad or wrong, lazy or unfocused."

As a child, Clelia could entertain herself for hours with fantasy, creating worlds and breathing life into her dolls. She reflected: "Fairy tales have always been a part of my life and have been a bridge for me into the other realm. I've collected them from an early age, and I wrote a paper on them in high school and another in college. My mother took me to see a wonderful collection of fairy tales in Georgetown, an enormous collection of international stories. Then I started buying fairy tales, little ones, new books, inexpensive ones. They are still on the shelf, along with von Franz's books. They have always been a doorway for me."

Angela was always a reader of fantasy, enjoying the battles between good and evil forces and the alternative spirits, places, and times, which capture the deeper truths.

As a child, I loved tales of fairies. These were not the traditional fairy tales, although I also knew and loved them. These were any stories of small, beautiful, mysterious, invisible, magical beings, and if they had wings and glittered, all the better. I could make them up and imagined myself part of this tiny community. For my fifth birthday, a dear family friend, who was like a Fairy Godmother to me, made me a blue and sparkly gold fairy dress with silver trim, surely to transform me into the blue fairy I so loved in *Pinocchio*. One Christmas, my mother dressed one of my dolls as a fairy queen, complete with stars on her dress, a crown, a scepter, and gossamer wings.

In my deepest child heart, I imagined myself to be a fairy, somehow far away from my homeland, and I easily disappeared into the landscape beyond the stories. Worlds opened up for me in a patch of grass or under a rock, where I could watch sowbugs move around in their dirty kingdom. Though no one ever knew the extent of my identification with this tiny, inner world, I am grateful for having been told the tales, sewn the dress, given the doll, and allowed to dig in the dirt.

As an adult, I find that I get insights when I least expect them. I walk in the park and experience a deep kinship with the people of all nations and languages who gather there, and I almost always have conversations with the Canada Geese and with Walter, the misplaced Muscovy Duck, as though we are old friends. Visions open up to me in the mountains as I look at the stars, when I notice a fragile wildflower growing through a crack in a granite cliff, a wound that is healing, or a forest regenerating after a fire: all are pointing to the inexplicable depth and wonder of creation.

The natural inclination to imagination, the pull to fantasy, and the use of imagery are consistent with how the literature describes the medial woman in her different roles. Janet Dallett, a Jungian analyst and writer who specialized in the psychology of creativity, wrote that artists have "an overriding need to give birth to the images and ideas that arise within."[64] Carol Pearson, an internationally known scholar and author, spoke of the magician-within as foreshadowing future events in our lives—in dreams, fantasies, and moments of intuitive insight.[65] These writers describe the energy of imagination of the medial woman by whatever name they may assign her.

Medial women have wonderful and unique gifts with a flavor all our own: empathy, broadmindedness, healing, truth-telling, and imagination. Each of us dances in and out of these gifts: opening them up and closing them down, touching and releasing, sharing and holding on. We need each other, and we need to be alone. We need the ordinary truths of the world, and the world needs the extraordinary truths we reveal.

THE STRUGGLES OF
MEDIAL WOMEN

Due to the permeability of the medial woman's character, she struggles in ways others may not. Here are some of the struggles that I've discovered are quite natural for these women, though they can work with and grow beyond them.

Becoming Overwhelmed

It is easy for medial women to become overwhelmed by the contents of what they are mediating.

Clelia experienced this when she was beginning to serve as a channel, for what was happening was beyond any of her previous experiences. She was receiving so much information, which she could not easily process, that she felt she must be going crazy. She began to control this by setting limits on how she would allow these forces to affect her, and she could continue to function in the world.

Elizabeth spoke of being driven in her writing by a very strong energy. "Sometimes I personify this into voices; at other times it comes as a vision. Sometimes when I'm writing, I get overwhelmed by the sheer number of voices that are saying, 'Write this, write this!' And so, I take a nap, I shut down. It's hard even to start. Those voices *want* to come forth. I've got to go with what comes through. There's even a sense of mission: got to do this! As a writer, I go for those highs when I can be outside of time. It is an amazing experience."

The force of the unconscious can overpower the ego of a medial woman and leave her out of touch with the material world. Wolff commented that the medial woman tends to lack the ability to differentiate between "conscious and unconscious, I and you, personal and impersonal psychic elements."[66] Mature medial women have learned the disciplines needed to contain the contents of the collective unconscious without destroying or denying them.

However, women who are less mature or less mentally healthy may sit at the border between sanity and madness. Most of us, at one time or another, have wondered where we are as we stand at a particular limen, and what it is that we need to communicate without misrepresentation. So, we have to work hard to stay grounded in reality.

Setting Boundaries

The quality of deep-seeing empathy contributes to and blends into the issues of being overwhelmed and struggling with boundaries. These are an intersection of the threads of the web. Many of us have much to say about the struggles with maintaining boundaries and our tendencies to lose our identities. This is natural due to the porosity of our souls.

Elizabeth said she always had trouble setting boundaries in relationships with people, tending to give too much. She learned to monitor how much she should say to any given person. However, it was hard for her to set the boundaries that gave her the time she needed to write and create. She often was so permeable and compassionate that she carried other people's feelings and problems, and sometimes had trouble distinguishing them from hers. She described herself as a *receiver*, going into groups and picking up on all that was happening, receiving all that was underneath. She told me, "One morning recently, I woke up just ready to tear heads off. I felt, 'I'm just going to write today, and I'm just not going to think about anything in this house that needs doing.' I get like that, and I've been able to tell my family, 'You won't like me if I'm not writing.' It's very freeing for me to know that maybe there's an archetypal reason behind my having such trouble setting boundaries."

Kathryn struggled with her perception that other people expected her to have no boundaries and be constantly available to serve them. She also had the experience of being sucked into another's psyche and had particular problems with this, especially when the other person was critical of her. She told me that she tended to lose her identity while understanding their feelings so deeply. However, she learned that for her work to be effective, she must establish some distinctions.

She said, "When I work with someone in prayer, it's *their* prayer, *their* faith that is important, not mine. Without feeling either dishonest or hypocritical, I will join them in things that I don't relate to at all. However, they must pass one test for me to work with them: whatever their belief is, it must be constructive. I just don't feel I have to fight evil."

Angela not only bridged the realms of the psyche, but she embodied one who crosses boundaries or holds opposites both physically, with her multi-racial heritage, and linguistically, as she easily and unconsciously took on another's accent or manner of speaking. People with many needs, whom Angela encounters both at work and home, could exhaust her. Yet, she experienced that the boundaries of time could completely disappear when she was with a good friend.

Clelia contended with the boundary issues in her response to the news, to people of poverty, to movies, to violence, to groups, and to psychic noise. She became overwhelmed when she indiscriminately picked up on everyone else's psyche.

Boundaries have been a challenge for me as well. At some early age, somewhere in my cells, I must have known that my parents had hidden inner wounds and great expectations of me. I had great expectations of myself, probably the inflation of childhood, and perhaps they were unconscious. I have no idea how old I was when I made a decision that most children don't make. I assumed that if I could only meet my parents' needs, I could heal their wounds. Even before my awareness of this dynamic took hold, I took on the role of supporting them, reflecting them, protecting them, and never abandoning them. One exception, however, was when I was six years old. I told my father I didn't want him to visit my classroom on the last day of public school week when parents had been invited to visit because no other fathers had been there. One look at the surprise and pain that crossed his face, and I reinforced my private pledge never to hurt or abandon either of my parents and to take whatever hurt they experienced upon myself because I could manage it. At six years old, I saw myself as an immense, strong container for their pain. Because of this relationship, I have developed the gift of listening behind words to wounds, and this I can offer to those who have sought me out as their pastor, therapist, or friend. That gift, however, has come with a significant price.

Boundary issues have also come up in my relationship with my mother, for as I used my ability to know deeply, empathically, and intuitively in response to her, I also had trouble distinguishing who *I* was as an individual. This carried over into my relationship with *Mother Church*. The expectations of ministry often seemed willing to step across boundaries that other institutions would typically never consider invading. There were no 9:00-5:00 hours in the church; there were no two-day weekends or holidays; we could count on few uninterrupted dinner hours; often phone calls woke us up; even the doorbell once rang at 4:00 in the morning by a person in distress. This called for maximum flexibility and sometimes the need to flee. Such flexibility is both the gift and the pain of ministering in the church, and my flexibility is both a gift and a source of wounding for me. I found the laws, ethics, and professional boundaries of being a therapist in private practice to be a great relief, for they were clearly spelled out. At the end of the day, I could almost always lock my file drawer and office door, drive home, shower off the day, and let it go, no matter what I encountered.

As I grow older and more aware of how I have violated myself because of lost boundaries, I am learning to keep margins tighter in many situations. I have learned that the power of "No" does not destroy a relationship. I have learned that voicemail can preserve a quiet dinner. I have learned that not every parishioner who has surgery early in the morning needs to be visited even earlier. I have learned that our home does not need to be used as an alternative meeting center, and that a free evening does not need to be filled. I have obviously struggled with boundaries and continue to grow wiser as I learn to hold them firmly and to see them as guardians of my soul, which is underneath and within my actions and good intentions.

None of us who are medial women claim to be the originator of what we mediate. If we did, that would become a boundary problem leading to inflation.[67] The boundary confusion that all of us experience may result from taking into ourselves the potentialities or responsibilities of others.[68] Or it may be that we have such psychic permeability that clear distinctions become difficult.

Certainly, Wolff recognized this tendency toward boundary confusion. She wrote, "The collective unconscious, by its nature, is not limited to an individual—a further reason why the medial woman identifies herself and others with archetypal elements. But dealing with the collective unconscious demands a steadfast ego-consciousness and a firm grasp of reality. As a rule, the medial woman has neither at her disposal; consequently, she creates confusion because she herself is confused. Conscious and unconscious, I and you, personal and impersonal psychic elements remain undifferentiated."[69]

A medial woman must have a strong and intact ego in order to be healthy and effective in her tasks and set boundaries without guilt. Strengthening and refining the ego must be part of her developmental growth, perhaps more for the medial than for any of the other structural forms.

Encountering the Mother Archetype

All the medial women I know have distinctive relationships with the mother archetype, different from the women claimed by the mother archetype as their primary way of being. Again, Wolff used words to describe the mother archetype that translate into the English words *caring, protective, supportive, giving,* and *instructive.*[70] The mother is drawn to everything that is undeveloped, in need of protection, or in danger, and to anything that must be cared for and nurtured.

The archetypal role of mother is available to all women, whether they are capable of bearing biological children or not, and many of us have found ourselves in the role of the mother as medial women. Some of us have struggled with this, and for some it has been a delight.

Angela found herself in the mother role not only with her own children but with institutions. She mothered troubled children and adolescents *in* institutions over the years, and she also mothered *whole* institutions, such as the adult parole facility she managed. But she got tired in the role of mother and found that it demanded that she be "on" all the time. Some of her mothering was expressed in the form of nurturing people's spirits and moving them forward in their insight and inner awareness. Some of Angela's mothering had a protective quality, as when she withheld the knowledge of her sexual abuse from her parents for fear that her own mother would be hurt and that her father would be so angry that he would kill the perpetrator and end up in prison.

Elizabeth observed that with her marriage, she inherited *his* mother. Her mother-in-law had the qualities of the all-giving, all-consuming mother, which were so different from her own mother's style of mothering that honored a place for her. She admitted that she struggled as an actual mother, particularly when her children were young. She shared, "When I became a mother, it was really a shock to find out that I wasn't suited to young children very well. The physical caring was almost beyond my grasp, especially with my depression. The fact that I had to attend to somebody every ten seconds was tough; I didn't realize how much time it would take to be a mom. It was a huge shift and relief when the kids crossed that point where they could go to the bathroom and get stuff out of the refrigerator themselves."

Kathryn found that people with whom she worked become emotionally dependent upon her and began to treat her like a mother, expecting her to be available for them at any time and to do things beyond her ability. Unless she drew the lines, she became an "emotional garbage dump," which did not enable her to channel deeper truths. The people she knew and with whom she worked were not always willing to have her draw clear lines, and they sometimes penetrated her private life in inappropriate ways. Because of her feeling that she must take care of everyone, she experienced total exhaustion. Ultimately, she learned how to be a channel of God's love and not to feel that she was responsible for taking care of the world on her own.

Clelia stated that she had a lot of the mother in herself. "As a matter of fact, some of my students used to call me 'Mother.' However, I've had a lot of struggles with this mother force: always giving a bit too much, always taking care of someone, and not knowing that I need care. I even take care of something before it's been asked to be taken care of. When there's a need, I tend to say, 'Yes.'"

I grew up living the mother archetype instead of having a place for the medial archetype to express itself and become embodied. I subtly mothered my actual mother from an early age and extended this mothering to whomever I encountered, especially to those who were disadvantaged in some way. I also had three younger brothers and was often responsible for some of their care. I know I'm compassionate and caring as the mother archetype is expressed through me. Still, like the others, I become exhausted in the efforts to meet unending demands and forget to mother myself. I totally loved being a mother to my children, although my journals remind me how much I also needed to be alone. As I mothered institutions, I tended to take too much personal responsibility and be so loyal that it was difficult to make the changes and decisions I needed for my personal care and sometimes for the institution's good.

My husband and I always worked together in the same church as a clergy couple, and we were often perceived as Mom and Dad for the whole church. One of the reasons I shifted to become a therapist was that the whole structure and process made everyone clear that I *wasn't* my client's mother. We could talk about their projections and what these might mean and also that I had clear boundaries that were never crossed.

Medial women are taken off guard when their relationship with the mother becomes edgy. As I've reflected on this, I can see several dynamics involved in this complex relationship between archetypes and people.

First, there are fewer medial women than women of other structural forms, so it is highly likely that most mothers are not medial and are unaware of this energetic quality in their daughters. As daughters, we may trail "clouds of glory" when we arrive in this realm,[71] but we are easily conditioned by our mothers, who may be clueless about who we really are, and our mediality is misunderstood, ignored, put down, or undermined. This is not necessarily our mothers' fault, as they truly have no sense of whom they are raising. However, a deep tension may develop between mother and daughter over time.

Second, the mother archetype is more aligned with what Jung called the feeling function than with the intuitive function that characterizes the medial. Sherlock's study found that 90% of mother-identified women preferred the feeling function, compared to 65% of the medial-identified women.[72]

Third, the medial woman, in her unique ability to empathize using her intuition and deep seeing, knows the needs of those around her, often before they, themselves, do. In her deep sense of accountability, she responds to them. However, if she has difficulty with boundaries, she does not easily pull back and thus becomes caught up in the ever-giving archetypal mother, whose shadow is consuming rage. I suspect that all medial women experience rage when there is an unceasing demand for them to be mothers in the outer world of need, when what they want to do is to speak their truth and then move into the quietness required by their own archetype.

The fourth reason for discomfort with the mother archetype is that the mother role continues to be the most commonly accepted feminine role in our culture. Since there are so few recognized roles for the medial person in our culture, a medial woman often lives in a role that is not congruent with her mediality. We all dwell in a time of transition from patriarchy to what we hope will become *gylany*, a word I love. It means becoming a society or culture that honors the feminine and women and provides equality for all. When the feminine is truly honored, a whole range of creative opportunities will open up. Since we are still in the patriarchy, however, the mother role is still the most prominent one that is honored and understood. Medial women become exhausted when they engage in too much mothering.

Fifth, the medial woman may feel unclaimed by any archetype. There is a difference between living through a social role and being claimed by an archetype. That which Wolff describes as a structural form is the *archetype* of mother or of medial, not the *role*. One may be competent in a role without experiencing the passion or energy that comes with the archetypal hold—a woman can be a mother without feeling a strong and pervasive pull toward the mother archetype. The result of this may be boredom, fatigue, and depression, or on the other hand, the discovery of who she truly is. When medal women open themselves to receive the call of the medial archetype, they are amazed that the energy, which had been lacking, now becomes available to them.

Here is a final thought on medial women and the mother archetype, and a mother/daughter story. As I've mentioned, though I was clearly in the mother role at the trial of my daughter's rapist, it was the medial archetype that allowed me to be there and to hang in. The mother and the medial actually worked together for me in that situation. Since the medial archetype is flexible, I have come to believe that the medial is like a basket that can contain other archetypes or archetypal roles when that is necessary. I found strength and discernment as the mother role was held within the medial archetype.

A few years after this trial, my mother died. During this dying process, the Alzheimer's Disease often caused her to forget that I was her daughter and that she was my mother, though somewhere deep in her heart, I believe she knew. Her last word on her last breath was, "E-la-ú-ba-ba." I kept trying to understand, and she kept repeating it, as though pleading that I know what she was saying. When I finally asked her if she was saying, "I love you, bye-bye," she nodded. I said, "I love you, too. Bye-bye." And she stopped breathing.

At the time of her death, the self I had known, steered by the mother archetype, was already waning, and at her death I let go of more of it. I've found that as I've been able to claim my mediality, I love my mother in a much different and deeper way, and I know she loves me for who I am now. She has no more fear.

Mother and medial, mother and daughter, and mother. The cycle goes on within and between us. May we move beyond fear and come to understand these complex relationships as gifts to one another.

Borrowing Guilt

Medial women take literal or imagined judgments about themselves from the outside deeply into their inner beings, personalize them and then feel guilt, even when the guilt is unfounded.

In the year after college, when I was back home living with my family during the time of dying, I experienced guilt whenever I tried to move beyond the immediate needs of family to meet my own young adult needs. A few decades later when I experienced burnout and depression in the context of the church, I found myself feeling guilty for not doing all that I could once do with joy. I could literally no longer respond to many of the needs of people, couldn't be with people, or even comfortably do the extroverted work of ministry. I could keep going, because I had a good *persona*, but I even felt guilty about that.

My research participants had a similar relationship with guilt. Clelia experienced feelings of guilt that came when she said "no" to a request to help, to serve, or to be in the world, especially since she retired and had more discretionary time.

Kathryn's sense of guilt also arose when she decided to draw a line that might say "no" to someone's expectation of her, in order to save something of herself.

Elizabeth learned early to blame or judge herself as wrong when she couldn't get things done in a rational, linear way. This tended to be often. She described the energy of her creative process as more like a stew or a sponge than a line.

When Angela had too many expectations placed upon her, she had to withdraw, and found that she was not as capable of being out in the world and tending details as she might otherwise have been. Whether this was in her work or with her family, she confessed that she did feel guilt, which also might be resentment.

Each of these medial women felt guilt when she did not meet expectations from within or without, imagined or real.

Ulanov refers to *inflated guilt* that appears when the medial woman takes as her personal possession the potentialities and meaning that belong to others, just because she perceives these. At the same time, she ignores what is her own "proper responsibility"[73] The struggle with inflated guilt ties closely to boundary issues and is indeed a dynamic which underlies the feelings of guilt that all these women experience. I call it "borrowed guilt."

Facing Conflict

Conflict and confrontation are difficult for medial women, which may be a result of their porosity of being, which has led to their ability to feel all sides of any contentious issue. All of these women expressed in one or another way that they do not want to hurt another person and that the distress of negative engagements is searingly painful to them.

Kathryn would rather carry her irritation with people inside herself than to confront those people directly, and she rarely expressed how she felt if that disagreed with another person's perception. "I felt tension with an elderly woman who is in my prayer group, and she hadn't caught on to my feelings at all, but there was no way that I wanted to have any sort of confrontation with an 87-year-old woman on oxygen, who was losing her independence." Kathryn went to great lengths to avoid confrontation and conflict and said that conflict could really tear her up. "My inability to confront may be caused by my seeing so easily the other perspective or what is driving that person."

Angela also commented on how tough conflict was for her and that she avoided it at any cost. She thought that due to the trauma of her childhood, she disappeared physically or emotionally when she was uncomfortable. To enter into conflict, she had to feel very safe and wanted to feel that everybody else was safe. If it was unsafe in any way, she couldn't be there. She commented, "I don't mind telling someone that they're an asshole and that what they did was absolutely horrible, as long as they know I love them to death, and I'm telling them this because I love them."

Elizabeth struggled with conflict in relation to a narcissistic and controlling co-leader in a community group and discovered that even the boundaries that she set to protect herself and others created intense conflict and became a power issue. She also had trouble acting authentically when someone saw *through* her, so she held herself in and did not become assertive. She strove to protect herself and others without hurting the other person and without appearing defensive or inauthentic. She too has carried much conflict within herself rather than expressing it outwardly.

Personally, I don't even like to be in the presence of conflict between other people, let alone be part of conflict myself. Though I'm competent at conflict resolution professionally because I create a safe structure within which to hold the tension, on a personal level conflict is hard for me. My dad often left the room if there were conflicts at the family dinner table. My mother occasionally stated *her* position in a letter left on the offending child's desk or pillow. An uncomfortable silence followed until the "wayward" one of us apologized and came around to agree with her, which could make for some awkward days. As I grew up, I would bear the tension of holding tight to any of my feelings that conflicted with another person's. It was easier to hold tight to my thoughts and feelings than face the possible hostility, hurt, or abandonment that might happen if I expressed them.

While we don't want to hurt another person, this abhorrence of conflict also relates to the deeper dynamic that we as medial woman face within ourselves as we live in two worlds at the same time. Janet Dallett resonated with this: "Creative people often find themselves crucified on a conflict between the requirements of everyday outer reality and inner life that screams to come out, *will* come out in one way or another."[74]

The medial woman finds it difficult to deal with the tension within her own being as well as the outer conflict between herself and another. The musician and artist Tad and Noreen Guzie understood this and wrote, "It takes a long time before a Mediatrix [medial woman] can peacefully live with integrity in both worlds, denying neither one."[75]

For the medial women who have a strong thinking function, there could be a different response to issues of conflict. For example, the medial person who functions as prophet puts forth with boldness a message that is likely to bring conflict and that is often not popular in the status quo. However, the prophet does not personalize either the message or the response. While the medial women I have interviewed do not prefer the thinking function, Toni Wolff herself might have had a highly differentiated thinking function. Toni, Emma, and C.G. Jung were by most accounts able to resolve the tensions in their relationship and coexist. Toni, however, withdrew when Jung abandoned her in later life.

Feeling Misunderstood

Medial women experience being misunderstood and mislabeled by those who think life is lived solely or primarily in the external and material world.

One of the first comments that Angela made to me was how sad and resistant she felt to the world's negative labeling of *any* person, including the medial person. Remember that Angela worked with women who have been incarcerated. She experienced the world projecting its craziness onto people who were different, including herself, and Angela found that she needed to spend enormous energy fighting against false impressions. "My tears come from the place of being unique and different in this world and not being valued for it."

Elizabeth shared that the way she thought might be alarming to some people and overwhelming to others, and she suspected that people felt uncomfortable in her presence. Her mother named her childhood intensity *depression*, and her father saw her tendency to be quiet and to daydream as *laziness*. She recounted: "I am aware that often I am misunderstood. I have a tendency to overwhelm my husband. Over the years, I've tried to share some of my sense of the unconscious with him, but it's really not fair. It does overwhelm him. He says, 'When I see it, when it materializes, when it's here in black and white, then I'll believe it.' I respond, 'No, I *know* that this is true. I just know it.' It's hard to be who I am and to live between these realms when one realm is so much more dominant than the other, when ordinary time and space are what most people see and understand reality to be. Life is really much more mysterious. So much of who I am is not reflected, honored, or given a name. When it is named, it's often negatively labeled. My nature is really misunderstood. I even wonder whether I want to be understood."

Elizabeth also confessed that she had trouble understanding and feeling comfortable with the experiences of some vivid medial people, who were different from the subtle medial that she was.

As a vivid medial, Kathryn felt that she didn't fit into the world. She found that people went as far as labeling her *evil,* were afraid of her powers, considered her *crazy,* or at the least saw her as *ridiculous.* She also expressed concern that many medial women may not develop their gifts because of their fear of what people will think of them. Kathryn commented that she doesn't "fit in very well to this earthly life." She saw herself with one leg on one side of the fence and one leg on the other. Of course, that is one powerful image of "medial."

Each of us has experienced in one way or another that she feels different and does not fit in with the world. Clelia and I suffered more than the "average duck" in getting our psychology licenses. I say this intentionally and with a smile. As I struggled with mastering the inner workings of test construction, statistics, and some concepts that I'd never even heard about, I was sure I would never pass the licensing exam. My analyst worked with me as I sought to conquer my anxiety about it and then said, "You are not a duck." He was referring to Hans Christian Anderson's tale of *The Ugly Duckling.* I used that as a mantra during that long, intense time of studying: "I Am Not a Duck." I asked a friend to make me some pins with a picture of a duck with a red line through it. Since that time, I have received beautiful figures of swans from people who know and love me. When I have been in seminars, I have heard over and over the importance of evidence-based psychology, and as one who appreciates science and grew up in the midst of a medical family, I am glad that there is such rigor now in my field. At the same time, in my heart I know that I stand on the spiritual side of the spectrum, rather than the measurable side of psychology, and I have to remind myself over and over again that I'm really not incompetent—"I'm just not a duck."

Clelia described what we both experienced in the testing process. "It could have been that I cut all that was medial in me off, because I had so much to do to get the license, to stay in that world, to study for those exams, and to get all those hours. But I felt like I was cutting a part of myself off, because it seemed that it didn't fit into that world. I needed to prove to myself that I could make it in the realm of psychology. . . . The process of getting the credential inflicted wounds on me."

You will be happy to know that we both passed with flying colors on the first try, and neither of us ever had to construct a test.

By not understanding my strong medial qualities and therefore repressing them, I have been left with the feeling that there is "no place" for me in the world. Yet my longing for a place was heard by the old man of the cave in my dream, who called me to the place where I am to live, a place with the turtles and snakes below the smoke-filled city at the entrance to the dark cave. And now, there would also be swans in their midst as well, but perhaps no ducks.

I recently came upon a set of letters exchanged between my mother and me years ago. With some fear and trembling, I had shared with her that I had been in analysis for some time and a bit about the nature of it as a journey deep within. Having forgotten this letter for 30 years, reading her honest response again brings forth a sigh of relief. She wrote, "I'll not pretend that I understand the depth and intensity of your yearning to explore 'the deep places of the spirit.' This will not surprise you because I'm sure you realize that I do not have the depth of understanding that would prepare me to appreciate what you experience, but I respect it as a gift that you have that didn't come through my genes." She acknowledged our differences and expressed respect for my way, without judging or pretending to understand it. I am touched more now than I even was then.

Angela also always felt she was different from the world. As a teen she felt she was "never really *in the world*" and still had to hold herself together "to be here in this world." She was most comfortable referring to those who live primarily in the upper-world as *they* or *them*. "I'm just different from the world."

Linda Leonard wrote, "Since her visions cannot be comprehended by rational thought alone, she threatens hierarchical thinking and is feared, ridiculed, and even condemned for her access to a realm that many refuse to experience."[76]

Creative vision is almost always incompatible with existing collective values. "Creativity brings forth images of new gods that challenge or destroy the old, while an established collective necessarily holds to the old gods."[77] Dallett considered that "a major—perhaps *the* major—psychological task of our time is to rescue the creative life of the spirit from destruction by the ossified patriarchal values and lifeless materialism that characterize a large segment of Western culture today."[78] Though the medial archetype has no exclusive hold on creativity, a well-functioning medial person is one who is creative and in this way is often also in tension with the established culture.

It is true that our visions are not comprehensible to the rational mind, and we may bring forth new gods, which always challenge old gods. This is the underlying trait of the medial woman and the reason why we feel different and misunderstood. This triggers the experiences described by all of us of being called *crazy, stupid, ridiculous,* or *evil,* and of having to spend enormous energy just showing up in the world, let alone fighting to be received. We experience fear beneath our experiences of being invalidated, of being judged, of withholding and cutting off our nature to be a part of the world, and of living out of a different archetype. It is hard to face being misunderstood.

Being Discounted

Being misunderstood and feeling discounted are intertwined threads that are common to medial women. Somewhere they intersect on the web of mediality.

Kathryn recounted that one of her deepest and most long-lasting wounds came early on in her work as a healer. She attended a mainline Protestant church, where she was active teaching Sunday School, and her children were in the youth groups. The minister and his wife had a child with an undiagnosed, traumatic illness related to epilepsy, which gave him seizures. When Kathryn realized that she was being called into healing ministry, she thought to herself, "I might be able to help this child." As she talked to the minister, she was heartbroken when his only comment was, "I have no belief in faith healing. If I had a toothache, I would go to a dentist; I wouldn't go into prayer." She became cautious and learned not to go beyond people's belief systems in her expressions of who she is and what she does. Sometimes when she shared something that came to her, she did so with fear and trembling, and it took all her courage. Kathryn lamented that our culture restricted her work. She couldn't teach much of what she would like to teach.

In my own childhood, I perceived my mother's power over me as a dismissal of my own taste, longing, and sensitivity. As an adult, I unconsciously allowed others to take similar power over me and experienced the same sense of being discounted. In my marriage, the opposite is true; we have shared our parenting, our ministry, our duties, our lives. I have always felt respected, free, safe, and real with my husband.

In ministry, one of my district superintendents asked what areas I wanted to work in with the church that I was serving. I shared my desire to work with more spiritual and pastoral areas rather than administration. He pompously responded that I only wanted the "whipped cream." Not only did he belittle my skills and interests, but he disregarded my deepest longing and call. Looking back on this, clearly it was a projection of his own inability to work effectively in these powerful areas of spirit and soul and of his own interest and skills in administration. His words became an echo of the church culture's valuing of administration, finance, member counts, and other tangible products and devaluing of the deeper rootedness and the connection with the holy. While I know that this is a somewhat skewed view, it shakes me to my core.

Each of us, as medial women, has experienced that we carefully reflect the needs and feelings of others while our own needs and feelings have rarely been carefully reflected. Those people who have been able to mirror medial women remain dear to all of us, and they are rare in our lives.

Wolff suggested that the medial woman can sense, activate, and sometimes represent to another person the archetypal base of that one's personality.[79] I imagine that if this insight is not carefully managed, it could threaten the other person and result in their denying the validity of what the medial is saying. We must be very careful.

The experience of being discounted is the curse of the mythic Cassandra, who had been given the power to foretell the future by the Greek god Apollo, with his expectation that she would love him in return for this gift. When she refused his love, though he could not take his gift back, in revenge he rendered her medial power useless by decreeing that her prophecies would never be believed.[80] It is no wonder that the drama written by Aeschylus, in which he told this story, was a tragedy for all involved.

This curse has subtly seeped under the skin of all medial women, for it is not just the truth that is discounted, but also the woman. Each of the women I know has had experiences of being belittled, not taken seriously, feared, ridiculed, condemned, controlled, proclaimed mad, criticized, silenced, exploited, diluted, scapegoated, stereotyped, and then dismissed without being truly known. The experience itself may not even be as traumatic as the dread of it, for we know it is coming.

Suffering Loneliness

Perhaps because of the discounting or misunderstanding by others, these women have spoken of their deep loneliness and have expressed delight as they received and claimed the name *Medial,* for if there is a name, it means that they are not alone. They are surprised to realize that and also to discover that they are neither crazy, stupid, nor despicable.

Angela commented that she was able to be in the deep center of herself and to trust herself to be in that place for other people. However, she was not able to trust many people to be with her at that deep place in the core of her being, except her therapist and one friend. Beyond these few, she was very careful to whom she entrusted this precious medial nature of her being. I felt privileged that she entrusted so much to me.

Kathryn acknowledged that it was difficult for her to share her experiences and the inner part of herself with others, even those whom she trusted and respected. She discovered that when she thought someone would understand and she took the risk to reveal herself, the other person often didn't value her. In talking with me, Kathryn took the risk that I would receive who she was without judgment. She intuitively knew which people might understand and came to realize that some of her most trusted friends just wouldn't. She said, "I tend to be a healer of healers, because I know what they're going through. I think I serve a good purpose in that regard; I'm sensitive to other healers, and I'm pleased to fulfill that role. However, I don't have a healer. I do have a wonderful husband, who stands by me and carries my feelings always. I've often been out on the front lines all by myself. I'd *better* believe in God, because often it's just God and me."

Elizabeth also spoke openly of her experience of loneliness, which she defined as the lack of people who resonate at the deep level that grounds and drives her. She experienced an emotional surge as we named the medial archetype. She had attributed her discomfort with people and her loneliness to the fact that there was something wrong with her, that she was shy or lazy. She also assumed that everyone felt this same loneliness. She was now able to say that her intensity and her need to work from the depths were not common to all people, and that others simply might not understand and cannot receive this quality in her. At her own core, Elizabeth realized that she was not lonely; the loneliness came when she was unable to find common ground with others.

I lived an essential loneliness growing up in a family that only saw part of who I really was. Death of loved ones brought a *soulful loneliness* as well as a great intimacy, for we were all face to face with eternal mystery, and everyone in my family was young at that time. All in the family were holding the loss and grief on a different level, and I clearly was in a supportive role then. However, it was hard to find those who were able to meet me at the point of my own needs and questions.

I felt the heightened *loneliness of isolation,* because I had been away and independent for four years of college. I finally did develop a trusting relationship with the youth pastor at the church in which I was working part-time during that year. However, my closeness to him became a threat to my mother, who was terrified that he was pulling me away from the family. In her anxiety, she mistakenly thought I was having an affair with him and insisted that I break off this friendship immediately. I felt that I had a choice between continuing a connection which nourished me, and was not romantic in the least, or continuing my relationship of support for my mother in a time of family crisis. I chose the family and my mother, of course. Thinking back, I realize that it didn't need to be an either/or choice. I was young then.

Medial women are lonely in crowds but have a home within ourselves that is a welcoming place. This external loneliness may come from fear, but that fear has come from the experience of being rejected, belittled, misunderstood, or dismissed. External loneliness is a product of our self-protection. We medial women admit to needing only a few people on the outside and a place of welcome at our deep center. Although loneliness is a wound in our lives, it may also be a wise choice.

TENSIONS WITH THE UPPER REALM

As a good follower of Jung, it's important I explore the dark side of the medial woman—her experiences of her tensions, wounds, and that which is dangerous to her. While this isn't fun, it's important "to hold the tension of the opposites" in order to find wholeness, and the shadow offers definition and dimension. So, here are some more of our struggles and stresses.

As medial women we tend to experience stress when it comes to the material, conscious, common areas of life. When we engage in these arenas, there is a cost to us that most would not recognize. In the following pages, I'll break this down a bit.

Institutions

Let's get back to our medial friends. As I've mentioned, all of the medial women I know have worked in institutional settings at one time or another, and all have made significant contributions. The qualities of responsibility, teamwork, perfectionism, sensitivity, and creativity are common, yet each one experiences tension in the realm of the extroverted, worldly collective conscious.

Being part of an institution is particularly difficult for medial women for many reasons. All of us have commented in one way or another that much of our work in administration and institutions calls for attention to detail, which we can all do, but on which we don't thrive. On some days we simply *cannot* do anything institutional.

Ironically though, medial women often find themselves performing with excellence in these areas of endeavor. They do this by using what Elizabeth called "a false front," and Angela named "autopilot" and a "professional *persona*."

Kathryn also spoke of her reservations about letting the people of her current church know of her administrative background. "If some of the people of the church knew about my administrative abilities, I can see where I would be taken off my healing path, and I would be heading up committees and doing detailed organizational work. If I get into all of the logistics of seeing that our meetings are publicized and keeping things on track, then I won't be doing what I really feel I'm supposed to be doing, which is right out on the front lines of the convalescent homes, hospitals, or the healing service. I want to stay centered in what I can do best, instead of what serves other people's perspectives of what they would *like* me to be doing."

Clelia identified that a danger for a medial woman serving in institutions is that the very qualities which she contributes to the common good are so valued and sought after that she can become stuck there. As she and I talked together, she offered a perspective that balances the value of institutions and the needs of the medial person. "As we become more conscious, we learn to put up with some of the world's institutions, because there is some good coming out of them.... We don't need to cut them off totally, but we do try to find another place where our medial nature can blossom, where we can live more creatively."

Elizabeth reflected that she always respected hierarchy and authority. "After college, I tried to learn everything my mother hadn't taught me about the business world, about wearing suits. I really wanted to try that on, so I went to work in the business world. I discovered that I could be very political and be very involved with what was going on, but it also felt like putting on a mask, trying to be something else. I'm a shape-shifter, but ultimately it came down to the fact that I just couldn't be in that world. Attention to detail isn't really my forte. I could make myself do it, but it's hard, very hard to do. On my lunch hours, I would go away and write in my journal. My writing exercise was to say, 'Okay, if I could be anywhere, where would I be?' It always came back to the fact that I would be at home, in a certain space, and writing. That's all I wanted to do. Every day I envisioned the space I would be in."

I have also discovered that institutions use me up. Sometimes I literally stop breathing, as I did in an internship at a clinic focused on sexual abuse. Shortly after I started work at this institute, I began to cough and then developed chest pain and deep wheezing. As I struggled over the months to catch my breath, it occurred to me that though this was certainly bronchitis, on a deeper level I was holding the breath of my soul as I tried to complete the volumes of paperwork, to do work I had not yet been trained to do, and to be surprised by unclear expectations that this agency had never expressed, all the while listening to the stories of women and children who had been sexually abused.

I have found that it is easy to adapt, and I tend to work harder and better until I forget my true nature and give excessive power to a current institution to define my life. The gifts of adaptation, excellence, and perseverance open the medial woman to becoming entrapped by institutions, yet often the challenge there dries up, and the medial woman becomes bored or burned out and chooses to leave.

The following words and phrases sum up the areas of tension that we all have with organizations: details, power, decision-making, constant tending, conflict, confusion, hierarchy, linear movement, false-front, persona, expectation, entrapment, adaptation, boredom, exhaustion, and burnout.

While all of us have experienced these tensions with institutions, none of us is willing to say that the culture can survive without institutions. Many people thrive in these settings, but we would rather not spend much of our time within them. One of the wounds of the medial is that there are few cultural roles for her, so she often ends up in an institution which doesn't utilize the gifts of her medial archetype in any professional way. It makes sense that we are most satisfied when we find a role that fits our dominant archetype, a tendency that underlines the longing of the medial woman as she searches for her unique and full place in an institutional culture.

Groups

Groups are also difficult for medial women. De Castillejo noted that groups can be not only difficult but also dangerous to medial women because they have a harder time knowing who they are than the women of other structural forms. "The mediumistic woman is always in danger of losing her own ego . . . in the group which claims her interest. She literally *does not know* whether it is her own interest or feeling she is expressing or that of the other."[81]

Clelia stated that she knew she didn't suffer from borderline personality disorder, but her boundaries could get lost so easily. "Obviously, I love people; my problem is that I have trouble being with them unless there is some kind of structure. Going to a cocktail party is absolutely horrible. I work well as a therapist one on one or with couples in therapy, but I could never do group therapy. I get totally exhausted in groups. I think sometimes there's too much psychic energy. I have to turn-on to be in a group or a party; a couple of glasses of wine helps. I can do this, but I'm totally wiped out afterwards. I think that when I'm in a space with a lot of people, I can't sort all the stuff that's coming in. I'm pulling in all kinds of noise that I can't sort out, psychic noise, not physical. I don't even realize at the time what I'm doing; I'm not standing there thinking, 'Oh, I'm picking up everybody's psyche.' I just get wrenched around and ripped up inside."

Kathryn felt socially inadequate in groups and survived by using a persona or by "faking it." This is how many medial women survive in corporate life. Like Clelia, Kathryn also felt exhausted and stressed from consciously or unconsciously being "on duty" all the time. This goes for social gatherings and parties as well. She "just can't process everything being in a crowd."

Elizabeth described herself as coming out of group experiences "in a frenzy. I've always been able to listen to people. I can be a very empathic listener when I choose to be, because it's easy to understand where people are coming from and what they might need. I may know their needs even more deeply than they do. I'm a little like a receiver. I go into a group and pick up on all that is going on. If I could only turn all that off! The experience is not just being open to others in the sense of talking, or saying things, or giving of myself; it's more like receiving *all* that's underneath. There's a deep sense of knowing about the dynamics." The experience may be creative and full, but it can also be overwhelming and leave her feeling manic or ill, since it cannot easily be contained.

I have experienced leading community worship as both exhilarating and exhausting and have needed to sleep for several hours after a Sunday morning in which I was in touch with hundreds of people, often on deeply personal levels. I have enjoyed and am energized leading limited retreats, as well as small, in-depth spiritual or prayer groups that incorporate silence. Some groups, however, can take on a form that becomes perilous when, for example, they take on a life of their own. Such was one long-term group in which I was a participant. It became chaotic at the end due to a variety of actions of the leader and an underlying malicious spirit that surfaced. The boundaries were breached, and the atmosphere became abusive. Fortunately, I had the resources to survive, but that was as close as I have come to soul-loss. It taught me to guard my own soul and those of others in groups with great care, and to be able to separate from the intangible dark spirit that may pull me in or draw me down. I also became well-acquainted with my own shadow in that experience.

Linda Leonard added that besides being confused and unsettled in a group, the medial woman may feel crazy. "Because the medial woman can feel unexpressed emotions around her and gain knowledge in this way, she often senses what is happening in the environment. . . . If the interactions in her . . . group or community are dysfunctional and crazy-making but are taken as normal by others, she may think she is the crazy one. She may pick up the stress of the family and act it out. Feeling weakened by the chaotic force of the unconscious contents that she mediates, and by the negative reactions of those around her, she can become isolated, hysterical, and paranoid and even sink into madness."[82]

All this says that medial women need to choose the groups in which they participate very carefully and to be sure that while they are picking up what is in the air, they do not abandon themselves to it. Our porosity leaves us exhausted. Not only are we in a group, but often we cope by masking who we really are.

Service

Being of service to another is laudable, and it is certainly at the heart of most faith systems. However, I'm not sure that service in the world is completely in sync with the nature of the medial woman, especially when it is undertaken in the extreme. This is a thread in the web that attaches to both the mother and the amazon archetype, once again making it three-dimensional.

Kathryn shared this of her experience. "Though I've never been pregnant, I've been mothering since I was 12 with all my nieces and nephews. When my own adopted children were small, my parents were getting into the limitations of old age; one of my sisters had cervical cancer, and my sister-in-law had thyroid cancer. I felt as though I was going to collapse because I was taking care of everyone. I was getting enough sleep, but I was just exhausted."

When Kathryn learned that she was clairsentient, she realized that this was why she was so tired. She discovered that when one is clairsentient, there is an energy that is separate from one's own physical energy, and whenever one is giving, it is this life-energy that is given. Our contemporary life is so disconnected from nature that those of us who give up our life-energy get more and more tired if we do not replenish it. It was then that she discovered that meditation is a way of replenishing this energy, and she began to meditate regularly.

I remember learning early in life that I was *not* to wait until I was asked before responding to a need; rather, I was to discern the need before it was even mentioned and to do something in response to it. My mother probably meant to teach me this in relationship to household duties, such as picking up clutter, sweeping a floor, or putting away laundry, rather than psychic needs of people, but I always applied that lesson more broadly. I tried to allay my mother's spoken concerns, to prevent issues that might come up, and to read her mind regarding what she had *not* said and respond anyway. Was it this teaching, or was it my natural medial qualities that led me to become highly intuitive in discerning others' needs? Probably both.

When my best friend of many years, Karen, found other best friends in eighth grade, a group into which I wasn't invited, my mother sat through many afternoons of my after-school tears and anguish. She finally suggested that I could solve the problem by going out the next day, standing up straight, looking people in the eye, and greeting them in a way that said I cared about them. I had grieved my loss long enough; now my purpose was to care about and serve others. She thought that, as a result, I might make new friends (I didn't any time soon). She thought that others would respond but that it shouldn't really matter whether or not they returned my care. It would be important to do this in order to move beyond my hurt feelings. I learned well that lesson and throughout my life performed the task of covering my hurts by focusing on care for the other. By the way, Karen and I later reconnected and have stayed the closest of friends over decades and thousands of miles. And she retains her close friendship with her other "best friends," to my delight.

I was one of a handful in college who continued to participate in church. Beyond attending worship, my connections with a loose interfaith college fellowship took me to dances with mental patients at the State Hospital on Sunday evenings, led me for week-ends to

Chicago and Milwaukee to paint tenement buildings, and even drew me to Mississippi in the spring of 1964 for a week of work in a African-American church, on which a cross was burned into the grass the night before we arrived. Eager to make a difference in the world, I found other service projects to do on my own as a college student, such as washing patients' hair in the hospital and tutoring children at the elementary school.

Spirituality and service have always been inseparable for me. As a young adult, I debated whether to be a social worker or a minister and decided to become a minister, though I knew no women in ministry. At that time, it seemed to me that social work would involve me in problem resolution, whereas ministry would allow me to work at the deeper levels of people's lives, perhaps even before problems developed. While the professions have changed over the years and my understanding has grown, I still remember that I didn't want to be a problem-solver of any sort. I wanted to encounter the soul of the other. So, I went to seminary to train for ordained ministry, one of the few women doing this at that time. That felt right.

After I went into ministry, I transferred my gift of deep listening and my tendency toward service into the church, *mother* church, which has a direct channel to *unending* human need. Together my husband and I served African-American, Mexican-American, Japanese-American, and international congregations, and had an intentional ministry with people who were deaf and had other disabling conditions. We enjoyed the stimulation of knowing many people on intimate levels. Our telephone lines and home were usually open, as were our office doors. Our ministry was lauded; we were loved; we were given larger churches with more administration, more human need. But it was too much.

Here's a story I wrote about one such moment:

A True Story: But Your Light Is On

Tuesday was one of those days when human need seemed to find its way to my office, over the phone, and into my heart from morning to night. It had already become dark when I was ready to leave; all the other staff had gone, and there came yet another knock on my outside door. I opened it, and there stood one of the street people we know and frequently help.

She wanted money; her check wouldn't be here until tomorrow. Since we don't give out money, to respond to such a request usually means that we take the person to Burger King and pay directly for a dinner, or follow them to the gas station and fill up a tank. Frankly, I was so tired, and it was nighttime. I simply said, "I really can't help you, and the office is closed right now." Without a moment's hesitation, she responded with one statement, which brilliantly captures the danger of ministry—"But your light is on."

Then there is the memory of Bernice. Bernice was an elderly woman, an activist on many fronts, who attended our church. It was a precious Friday afternoon. I say "precious" because that was our one day off, and often we didn't even get that. My husband and I went to a movie. The theatre was across from the State Office Building, and Bernice and others were picketing in protest of something. We waved when we saw them as we went into the theatre. The following Sunday, Bernice verbally ripped us up and down right by our office door, in front of God and everybody. "How dare you go to a movie when there are significant social issues that need your attention!" I always felt a little sad for Bernice, when I wasn't resenting her constant judgments of us. Her life wasn't much fun.

How does Bernice's confrontation relate to my mediality? I suspect that most people would have pushed back at that moment of hostility and cried out their own names into the universe. I didn't; I couldn't risk doing so. I felt intimidated, thoughtless, stupid, negligent, and bad. I felt judged.

That Friday we did tend our souls and didn't cross the street to join in that protest. Yet, how many other times did I allow myself to cross such a street, to cross over into my mother's skin, into the church's skin, into the skin of others, into the skin of judgment, into the skin of other protests, into the skin of endless suffering? I often used my ability to know deeply, empathically, and intuitively in order to respond to needs, suffering, and life situations right in the moment. The one secret that I did keep from myself and from most others was how profoundly I had cut off my own soul, my own deep wants and needs, my own perspective and gifts. Had I sold my medial life in exchange for love and acceptance? Or was I afraid that the *other* would take the fact that I stood up for my personal needs as a sign of my selfishness? How could I not have known the price I paid? All for a Friday afternoon movie.

Complexity

A young Roman Catholic, at the time of his ordination as a priest, wrote these words:

We are simply asked
To make gentle our bruised world
To be compassionate to all
Including ourselves,
And in the time left over
To repeat the ancient tale
And go the way of God's foolish ones.[83]

"We are simply asked." Simply. Let's turn to that one word, perhaps the one word that could truly feed our souls.

We live in a complex age, in complex environments, and we adapt to this the best we can by becoming complex ourselves, by multitasking, and by juggling all the balls of our lives. I for one have always had the tendency to make things more complex than they need to be, probably because I struggle to make sense out of the material, linear, detailed tasks before me. My mother used to tell me that if there were a harder way to do anything, I would find it.

I had a terrible time with details, which was probably why I wasn't good at math and had problems memorizing the History of Western Civilization in college. Plus, I don't really care about memorizing dates, places, numbers, and names, but I do remember everyone's birthday, because I care about them.

Details: no matter how hard I have tried to master and perfect them, they have always tripped me up. I actually can now laugh at how silly these mistakes were, but at the time they felt devastating, and if given the chance I would probably make them again.

- As a "seamstress," I tended to sew the legs of the pants together in front and back, so they looked more like a weird skirt.

- More than once, I made and froze a pie crust. When it came time to serve it with fresh fruit, I forgot to bake it first. That was a real issue when my mother and my husband's parents came for Easter dinner one year, and I served a delicious strawberry pie on an unbaked crust.

- The title page of my dissertation reads, "Doctor of Philoosophy." I should have noticed the spell check on that one, but it was also missed by my $800 proofreader and my three committee members. Only my niece found the error as she was perusing it after it was published.

Oh my, embarrassment! I make mistakes with details all the time and experience shame or guilt, depending on how bad they are. Caught in the world of details, I often go the way of foolishness.

Complexity: there is often a simpler way, and I always tried to find it, though it most always turned out to be harder. As the oldest of four kids, my childhood job was to fold the laundry. Every day after school a huge pile of laundry was waiting on my bed to be folded and put away. I liked to fold, and worked carefully at making the folds neat and the clothes flat. But I hated putting the laundry away and making all those trips all over the house, opening doors and drawers, fitting my neatly folded laundry into whatever else was already filling that drawer or closet. So, in an effort to avoid so many trips, I became creative and developed what I thought was a simpler way to do the job. I started to pick up *all* the piles at once and stack them on top of each other, and then carry them all on my head off to their destinations.

Inevitably, I would drop the whole load. Inevitably, my mother would come upon the scene about the time I was scooping her clean laundry up from the floor. Inevitably, she would tell me that there was another way to do this, a simpler way. Inevitably, I would do it the same way next time.

Recently, I found a wonderful definition of simplicity that just seems to fit. The word "simple" comes from the root "plex," which means to fold. Words like multiplicity, duplicity, complicity, and complexity suggest images of material spread out with many folds, two folds, all folded together. Simplicity means "to spread out without folds." To be simple is to be free-flowing, unimpeded, not caught in folds or pockets, not sidetracked, not inevitably finding the hardest way. In fact, as a child, I always suspected that the simplest way would be not to fold the clothes at all.

The paradox for me is that folding clothes is hardly a complex task in the usual way of thinking, but it is a very *material* task. It is in the physical world of sewing, folding clothes, baking pies, typing flawlessly, and so many other mundane tasks that I, as a medial woman, just get it wrong. Navigating the complex material world is not my preferred or most natural way of functioning. And so, caught in the world of complexity, I excel in creating more complexity. I always do.

I believe it is in the *simple* that the depth and presence of mystery can be revealed, perhaps because nothing is folded around it to hide it, and one can see the whole.

Media, Noise, and Violence

All of the medial women I spoke with struggle with and often reject the media. None can tolerate the noise and violence.

Angela commented, "I have a huge problem with how the world communicates. Movies are hard, especially documentaries. I can barely sit through a documentary-type film; it is difficult to handle at my core. I am enraged at the end, and I feel impotent. I'm not the fighter, the amazon. I'm just unable to tolerate the media's noise and violence. I don't trust the newspaper; I don't *read* the newspaper; I don't listen to the news; I can't stand it. They put nothing but bad information in it most of the time. I do read the book section."

Clelia spoke of her similar response in this way: "Whether it is deep empathy or loss of boundaries, I sit in the living room and try to read the morning paper and start crying. There is so much pain. The same thing happens when I watch television; so, I usually don't watch news on television because the visual is even worse. Somehow when I see all these disasters going on, a part of me is there. I don't go to movies and haven't for many years. When I was a child, I would not go to a movie unless my parents assured me that nothing would be nasty. It's been that way all through my life. I monitor what I take in. I don't want that brutality to come into my life. I've walked out on movies because there's too much violence. I feel like I have to get rid of the violence, the noise, to cleanse it from my being."

Elizabeth commented on how media and noise interact with the porosity of her soul. "Sometimes what is in the environment is painful, and I am filled with pain because I've taken it all in. For example, my husband often brings home videos that I just can't watch. He can watch them, get the thrill, and then turn them off. I can barely watch, and I usually get angry. 'You're bringing that into bed?' The television actually isn't in the bedroom, but it just as well could be. I long to tell him, 'I don't want to be with you if you watch that movie. I don't have the tolerance. I don't want you carrying that in here. I don't want to be *around* you after you've watched that for a few hours. It just seeps through.' I don't know how to tell him all this."

Kathryn also spoke of this. "I have a difficult time with noise and violence. I decided that I would visit my only remaining aunt every year. One of her sons, who was widowed, came to live with her, and he was fascinated with television violence. I didn't realize there were so many of these programs on TV. He would go from one to another; they were all shooting, sirens, and fighting. He had them at a very high volume. I went to bed every night completely unnerved from the noise and the message of the programs. Noise and violence are hard for me to tolerate."

We have all wept over the news because it penetrates so deeply into our beings, and sometimes when I take in too much, my creativity freezes. I tend only to open up to public radio or television, as there are no commercials and the news is balanced and not sensational, though still often horrible.

While we lived in Berkeley in the late '60s, everything was in upheaval, including our seminary, and the world seemed hostile. While I loved living in Berkeley, I could neither tolerate violence nor handle conflict. Walking across the University of California to a class on the other side of the campus, my husband and I encountered students protesting the Vietnam War and the National Guard standing in lines facing them with tear gas. When the masses moved and the tear gas filled the air, my husband and I were separated. He ran on through the middle of it all to class. I turned back. Perhaps this was due to my low tolerance for violence, or perhaps it was due to just plain terror. He has always helped me censor films before I watch them, especially those with emotional violence, which are difficult for me to bear. I leave if there is physical violence. The noise, rapid pace, canned laughter, and flashing colors of television are more than I wish to subject myself to, and as a result, I rarely watch television. I also don't enjoy the noise, competition, and energy of athletic games, even though they are not intentionally violent.

The media reflects our contemporary culture as it embraces sound and violence. However, what is happening in the psyche of people steeped in this may not yet be fully known or appreciated.

Part of our suffering as medial women comes because we stand at the edges of Western culture. We can threaten the culture, since society has little place for psychic events and deep sensitivity. Yet it is also our experience that the culture can produce fear in us. We cannot contain the energy of the action, noise, and violence that is part of everyday life and permeates our beings, and we have trouble allowing all this to slide off us in the ways that others can. The medial "may see too far and too deeply into the unconscious to be comfortable for those around her,"[84] but she may also "see too far and too deeply into the unconscious" to be able to handle the disregard of people for other human beings, for all life, and for the earth.

WOUNDS OF THE MEDIAL WOMAN

All people experience wounding. It is part of being human. What follows next are the wounds of the medial women with whom we have been journeying. These strands of the web interlock with the struggles and tensions we experience.

Fear

Our medial friends all have fears. Though they could not be classified as worriers, each carries strong fear of particular things.

Elizabeth, the writer, feared publishing as much as she longed for it. This fear ties in with her fear of persecution and of closed-minded and bigoted people who are prone to attack others. At her core, she felt her vulnerability and the vulnerability of her family if her writing were to become public. Her fear of those who will attack was so strong that it blocked out her anticipation of any positive responses that would undoubtedly be there when her material was published. Elizabeth also had a deep fear of flying, heightened following her brother's death in a plane crash.

Clelia also admitted to a fear of heights, precipices, and flying, which she endured simply to get where she wanted to be. She experienced fear that led to panic when she heard a train whistle or saw railroad tracks. As both a child and an adult, Clelia struggled with fears and terrors, and she had not figured out why these irrational fears were part of her life.

One of Kathryn's fears was that she would fail to express to others what had been revealed to her. She sensed that she came into the world for the purpose of channeling information from another realm, but it was so difficult to find the avenues for expression that she feared she might not be able to do all that she was called to do. Part of her longing was to publish more than she already had.

Angela's profound fear was abandonment. In part, this stemmed from a betrayal by her closest friend. She vowed never to get that close to a person again because the pain was immense.

Like all people, my fears took place in a variety of contexts. Here's an old but true story that helps me with my fears to this day.

A Story from My Childhood: Michael Rymer

When I was a little girl, about six, I walked home from school each day.

It was great fun
splashing in puddles and sinking up to our boots,
smelling flowers,
and finding treasures.

It was great fun until … Michael Rymer discovered me …

Michael Rymer was a boy who lived around the corner from me. He was about my age, and he also walked home from school.

What Michael discovered about me was that I would believe anything.
     And so …
          Before long …

"You know—a witch lives in this house.
She watches for little girls,
and she comes out and kidnaps them
when she sees them."

And so—every time I came to that house,
     I bent down low beneath the fence and scurried past on my hands and knees.
     Michael just walked past.
     Witches must not have cared about boys.

One day on the way home from school,
Michael Rymer discovered that someone's red mail flag
had broken off.

"You know—when these aren't attached to mailboxes,
they become hatchets.
They slice people up.
That's why they are painted red: blood."

And so— as Michael waved the hatchet in the air,
I ran home as fast as I could.
                    To save my life.

In those days
            Weeds grew up through the gravel in the park by
our house. One spring day, while we were in school, the city
trucks sprayed the weeds with oil. Yuck! What a terrible smell
as we walked past the park.

"You know—that's poison they spray with.
If you breathe even a little bit,
you will die by tonight."

And so—as I ran past the park,
I held my breath,
guaranteeing I would be alive for another walk home
with Michael Rymer the next day.

That night after dinner
I told my father for the first time
how I risked my life each day walking home from school.
Actually, I cried a little,
because I was really a little scared of what could happen.

"But Michael Rymer is teasing you,"
My father told me in his grown-up voice.
"He's having fun making you scared.
Tell you what: you fool him. Tomorrow whatever he says
to you, you say back,

'Michael Rymer, go peddle your petunias!'"

Whatever that meant, I was determined to say it.
I practiced in my mind all day saying,
"Michael Rymer, go peddle your petunias!"

"You know," began Michael Rymer, pulling a toy fire truck from under his jacket as we neared the park.

"You know—this fire truck can squirt real water, and it comes out so fast that it will knock you down."

And so—I said, in my best Daddy voice as I walked tall and straight, "Michael Rymer, go peddle your petunias!"

"What did you say?" asked Michael Rymer.

"Michael Rymer, go peddle your petunias!"

The only times I saw Michael Rymer after that were as I walked straight and tall past his house while he was playing with his dog, Red Rock, in his yard.

Maybe Michael thought that's what "peddling his petunias" meant.

Beyond Michael Rymer, as a child, I also feared death, especially the death of my family. Interestingly enough, having faced the experience of two of my immediate family dying at young ages within a year, the privilege of being with people in their dying process is now one of my greatest strengths and passions. I loved hospital chaplaincy work and would have been a good hospice chaplain. Over the years, in supporting my mother, who worried about many things, I have learned to live with relative calm related to catastrophic reality. My deepest fears come from my inner sense of inadequacy and relate to rejection.

Fear is undoubtedly not a feeling limited to medial people, but the medial women I spoke with have all experienced fear. *Fear* is also frequently used in the literature on medial women. In some cases, medial women are afraid of the power of what is coming to them from the collective unconscious. This has not been an issue for these five women, for the most part. Some of the apprehensions of these women relate to their sense of being overwhelmed by the culture of rapid travel and unrestrained violence, their fear of not being able to produce what is calling to come forth, the fear of inadequacy in the outer world, the fear of abandonment, and the fear of going crazy. Our friend Linda Leonard knew this when she wrote, "Visionaries often fear going mad themselves. Drifting away from earthly life via dreams and visions is a danger that can end in madness."[85] We have all spoken of the experience of fearing madness, though all of us have had strong enough ego structures to manage the dislocation that we were facing.

Though the centuries-old persecution of witches has not been part of my study, this is an important area to consider when we think of the utter maltreatment, intimidation, and destruction of medial types throughout the Western world. The fear that the medial person feels in her bones may be grounded in generations of annihilation of her nature, another curse that has seeped under her skin.

Afflictions

The medial women I researched tended to carry what was around them in their bodies. One might assume that when Wolff described the task of the medial woman by saying, "She must express or act on what is 'in the air,' what the surrounding environment cannot or will not admit, but what is there nonetheless,"[86] she might have meant bodily as well as psychic expression.

Clelia had constant body issues throughout her life, including several near-death experiences as a child. Sometimes she could attribute illness to stress; sometimes she became ill when a person close to her became ill. She had spinal surgery, continuing back pains, and fibromyalgia. Through illness, which caused her temporarily to leave what she had been doing in the world and tend her body, she was able to identify significant changes that needed to be made in her life and decided how to make these. Clelia learned of the close connection between body and psyche, and though she did not try to control her body through her mind, she respected and was open to the relationship.

Angela also had a lot of illness and was aware of the connection between body and soul. She tended to respond to what was happening by physically revealing it. Her daughter once experienced a traumatic event, and Angela's grief expressed itself unconsciously in an asthma attack so severe that she couldn't breathe and ended up in the hospital. Back pain, exhaustion, ulcers, and insomnia are all expressions of her body that Angela experienced and attributed to taking into herself what was in the air.

Elizabeth also carried her concerns for other people in her body since childhood. She responded to stress by becoming ill. She, too, experienced severe allergies to whatever is "in the air," a physical manifestation of the psyche of a medial person. Having an opportunity to be ill every few weeks as a child gave her a legitimate way to find the solitude she needed to re-group. She laughed when she said it was hard to find the time to be sick as a mother.

Kathryn discovered that when she was overwhelmed with more than she could process, she became physically ill, which often took the form of a bladder infection or a backing up of energy. She, too, experienced fatigue so deep at times that the tears ran down her face.

I also sometimes carry the illness of the environment in my body. I wonder now whether the severe curve in my back as a child was scoliosis/polio or the reflection of my psychic inability to stand straight and claim my own being. As I've previously mentioned, when I was an intern at a center relating to sexual abuse, I had severe bronchitis and couldn't breathe. Sexual abuse takes my breath away literally.

It would be impossible to separate out how much of the illness and physical distress of the medial woman is typical to all people and how much is due to her unique characteristic of taking on what is in the environment, even that which is toxic. Body and Soul are closely connected.

Leonard spoke of the body as she wrote of the visionary, saying that she must devote herself to her crafts and bear "the creative tension between the transcendent vision and the limits of embodied work." She must care for her body and the earth, and pay attention to the needs of society and the sensate world.[87] This is a difficult task for medial women, who are often disconnected from the sensing world, but a necessary balance.

Depression

All of the women I interviewed had experienced depression. For most of them, the experiences of descent and depression were connected strands on the medial web.

Elizabeth commented that in the journey of medial people, there are places beyond reason and understanding to which she must be open. One must go *through* the sense of loss and darkness one encounters rather than try to get out of it. Elizabeth moved into this part of her journey in the intense months after the plane crash that killed her brother, during the nearby Loma Prieta Earthquake, and also through her second pregnancy, all of which occurred in near proximity. She recounted being barely able to function, manage life's routines, or make decisions. She knew that she was on the edge of a mental breakdown but continued to live through the chaos, the unknown dimensions of darkness, and the inability to take control. Her creativity was heightened during this time, and as she wrote of her experience in the darkness, a book emerged.

Kathryn's depression came during menopause, and she was open to seeing it as both hormonal and part of her medial nature. There were days when she could not get out of bed and times when she found herself in tears with no particular precipitating event. During her depression, she allowed herself to be dependent and give up the idea that she could control her own body. She found the depression led her into deeper sensitivity to others and herself.

Angela also experienced depression but reframed it from being defined as clinical depression to representing a spiritual *staying-under*, which does not have negative clinical implications.

I also went through years of darkness in mid-life, characterized outwardly by depression, though perhaps rather than being a disorder, it was my journey into wholeness. Like Elizabeth, I could barely function through the daily routines that had once been so simple, and I certainly struggled with the role of ministering to the spiritual needs of others, let alone administrating, preaching, performing community service, and the extroverted demands that were constantly upon me. My depression may have been related to burnout. On the other hand, it probably was my soul's way of beginning to claim my medial self. It may have reflected the unspoken, early childhood feelings of hopelessness that I would never be able to live as the person I truly am. This realization through depression was a tectonic shift and left me shaken.

During this dark time, my qualities of extroverted serving diminished, and the true introvert I am emerged. In this time of dislocation, there arose feelings of guilt, for I could no longer respond to needs as I once had, even those that *were* spoken out loud. I couldn't be with everyone and connect with all their distresses, which had seemed to be the expectation of the job of ministry. At this time, I could barely share my own spirituality or be with others in theirs. Suddenly, I needed my home to be a place of refuge, separate from the people of my ministry. Suddenly, I did not want to do the management, preaching, and service of ministry. Suddenly, I went into a dark night of the soul, a deep life-abandoning depression.

The only literature I have found on depression of the medial woman is offered by Laurie Layton Shapira, a Jungian analyst who has written about mythology, and in particular about Cassandra, as this relates to psychology. Her volume explores the immature medial woman's difficulty in translating the darkness of the collective unconscious. "No wonder she is not believed. She cannot even afford to believe herself; her ego cannot accept what her shadow knows."[88] The women I have come to know are all mature medial women, whose egos finally accept, or at least acknowledge, their shadows. However, this acceptance does not make moving through the darkness easier; it only gives it context.

Disappearing

Each of our medial women confessed that she coped with the world by going undercover with her dominant qualities.

Clelia found that to function as a psychologist, she had to cover up who she was and ask those who knew her medial nature to forget that part. She continued to feel that she would have been judged and have trouble receiving her license if the powers of the psychological profession had known of her mediality.

Elizabeth responded to being misunderstood by covering up who she really was. "Yet when I'm in a situation where I have to put on a false front, it really kills me."

Kathryn actually used the word *undercover* to describe one of the areas of her wounding. "I spent 17 years in places where I've never felt fully at home." At the time of our conversation, she had found some places to use her gifts of mediality, but still, very few people knew who she really was and what she really was about. She was still undercover. She understood that if she were to share beyond a person's belief system, it would close down that other person's response to her, so she found it safer to maintain the relationship by remaining undercover.

It is not surprising from the literature that the medial person is a threat to the culture. Linda Leonard commented, "The Visionary seems dangerous because she sees things from the 'other side.' If her visions seem mad, it is because they turn expected routines and assumptions, we take for granted, upside down into chaos."[89]

Less has been written about the threat of the culture *to* the medial person. It is a tremendous loss to the culture when medials have to go undercover or are not able to develop their unique gifts, but the experience of going undercover is a direct response by the medial woman to the threat *from* the culture. Ulanov addressed the sadness and danger in this for the woman. "False doing arises from interruption of being. Instead of possessing a continuity of being from which a vigorous and unforced doing flows naturally . . . we suffer a crumbling at the center of ourselves. Our being has been invaded, taken over by alien elements, and exists now only in fragments. We are not seen or reflected back to ourselves and thus no true self forms at the core."[90]

How do we encounter the forces of the world? When we don't believe in our unique selves, we often cope by losing touch with our medial intuitions, developing a false *persona*, shape-shifting, playing a role, or living from another archetypal form. Although active and contributing to the world, the medial women I know also have learned to protect themselves in the outer world by going undercover.

THE DANGEROUS DARK PART

Being a medial woman isn't easy, but worse than what it isn't is what it is. There are many "dangers, toils, and snares," to quote an old hymn. Here are a few, interwoven with the medial's struggles, wounds, and tensions.

Facing Evil

Medial women are vulnerable to the dark forces of the collective unconscious.

Elizabeth stated that the medial journey, beyond reason and understanding, inevitably leads through the experience of loss and darkness. She was convinced that writers like herself, must deal with whatever they encounter on this journey to look into the face of light *and* darkness, beauty *and* ugliness, good *and* evil. Elizabeth experienced darkness opening up into evil, and she described the frightening experience of being slowly absorbed into a complex relationship with a person whom she came to believe was transmitting evil energy and embodying a destructive, dark power. During that time, she had difficulty asserting herself, protecting those for whom she cared, setting up appropriate boundaries, and still not hurting the one who projected such a dark spirit. This difficulty came from Elizabeth's medial porosity. If she were an amazon, she believes that she would have engaged in an open conflict, a classic battle between the forces of good and evil. Elizabeth recognized the shadow in herself and others and was uncomfortable with polarizing good and evil. Her dreams portrayed her concern about dark forces invading her basement, her deep inner life.

I also have experienced a darkness that borders on evil and can permeate my being. Sometimes this has been in the form of a powerful person; sometimes it has come in the form of a situation, such as the increasing darkness of the courtroom as justice was being subverted. In such times, I have had to leave and come back to my core being in another setting or with trusted people before re-entering and being present to the darkest of dark evil forces. Otherwise, it would be overwhelming to my soul.

Angela's permeability also opened her to dark spirits. As a child, she was as aware of the dark forces under her bed as she was aware of the angels in the corners of her room. Her grandmother honored the reality of this terror by looking under the bed and in the closet, and in doing so, honored Angela herself. When Angela came face to face with true evil in the form of sexual abuse by her stepfather, it was so powerful that she psychically disappeared. She longed to kill the perpetrator, but could not even bring this longing to consciousness until after his death.

Kathryn defined evil as a lack of awareness. She understood that her call as a channel was to offer awareness. She protected herself and others by focusing only on God and working only with people who wanted to work constructively. Evil to her was not an independent entity that she was called to fight. If she encountered dark spirits, or the playful, mischievous poltergeists, she invoked the authority of God and sent them on their way. And yet, Kathryn, herself, had been called *evil* by those who feared her qualities.

Medial women have an unconscious tendency to transmit another person or the culture's shadows and tensions. Poet and activist Eleanor Wilner shared these insightful thoughts: "When society itself is sick, the member most sensitive to the powerful disintegration in the air often becomes the carrier of that tension and the agent through which its resolution may be effected."[91] Medial women carry that tension and have spoken about their efforts to resolve it or to continue to live with its presence. All of these women I know have been able to differentiate themselves from the negative without being destroyed by it. As I write this, I also remember with honor those women called witches from centuries ago who were totally destroyed by it. However, whenever we have lived, each one of us has been profoundly affected by her encounters with that which is malevolent, and she has moved with caution in its presence.

Merging with Another

The issue of merging with another was huge for me growing up. It's similar to the struggle with keeping good boundaries and the gift of empathy, which are interlocking strands on the web. My psyche is so porous that it is easy to take on that of another person or the cultural milieu. As a child, I was deeply merged with my mother in a loving way, but I had difficulty individuating from her. One dream captures my sense of our relationship perfectly. In the dream, she and I are in my first-grade classroom, where an x-ray is being taken. It is a machine for two; she is in the front, and I am in the back. Throughout my childhood, I had an unconscious sense that while two, we were one. That changed consciously when I married, but that unconscious joining with my mother was a large part of my analysis as I worked at individuation. I hope my work freed her from this merger as well.

Surely, neither of us was aware of this. She was not cognizant of the ways this hurt me, understanding herself to be of a good-humored, practical, loving, observant nature. And she was. However, she was fond of telling me about my birth on each of my birthdays. "When you were born, the doctor held you up and said to me, 'You have a beautiful baby girl.' I took one look at you and replied, 'She doesn't look like much to me.'" She would have felt that I was being petty, small, and humorless had I told her that hearing this every year hurt me, so I bore it in pained silence, assuming that maybe I still didn't "look like much" to her. I did gain some perspective on that as I came to expect it each year, and I know that most new babies "don't look like much" when they first emerge, so I should never have taken that literally. However, there was an underlying sad feeling that lingered.

As a child, I had to wear brown Oxfords because as a girl, my mother only wore inexpensive mail-order shoes which did not fit, and her feet always hurt. There was no middle ground for me to wear shoes that fit and that I also liked, like other girls wore. She assumed that my feet were a reflection of her feet. I take secret pleasure when my daughter says that her own feet are one of her beautiful features, and I laugh to myself when I look at the Oxfords that she actually *chose* to buy one year because they were in style. No one will ever get me into Oxfords!

My hair grows forward; my mother's hair grew back. Rather than work with the natural direction and strength of my hair, she insisted that I pull it *back* the way she wanted it, out of my face, the way hers grew. She justified this by saying she was "training it to go in the right direction." I wanted my hair long and beautiful; she wanted my hair short and tidy. It was always short and tidy.

My mother hated lace and liked plaid. I loved lace; I wore plaid. However, I should add that she created the most beautiful lace formal for my high school graduation dance and helped me find a beautiful lace wedding dress. I now look at some of my childhood pictures, remember how ugly I felt, and notice how self-conscious I looked. There were no alternatives; I quietly bore the task of reflecting her perspective. I did not want to hurt her—ever. I believed that to love meant never to hurt another.

I remember being constantly on guard, beyond what a child should have to be. For example, when I was eight years old, she confided in me her detailed concerns about my brother, who was six, who she thought might be showing signs of obsessive-compulsive behavior and thought that he had fallen in love with his first-grade teacher. I was eight and had no idea what to do with that information, but I was her confidant.

Through the years of my childhood and early adulthood, I heard the details of her endless worries and conclusions about the family members, concerns that I should never have heard and that were often groundless. These were not just passing concerns, but fixations that went on endlessly and melded from one to another. Sometimes there was something to them, but often not. Nevertheless, I carried her worries throughout my childhood, unable to do much except listen and clear the way for her action.

I felt I could never be truly at peace when my mother was troubled. I believed I had no right to go about my life if hers was torn apart. I thought that my well-being depended upon her well-being. In many ways, I became her guardian, her shadow, and her mirror, all in the name of love.

After I left home and married, I continued to carry her concerns through regular letters, but much more at a distance. Though I invited her into our home, I never invited her into our family's personal life, because the worst thing I could imagine would be to have my family become the object of her worry or judgment. I had a tender and loving husband, a healthy marriage, and wonderful kids, and I didn't want any outside judgment or worry imploding on this.

Ann Ulanov warned of this danger of merging with others when she wrote, "If objective contents in herself or others are taken personally or misunderstood, the medial woman may feel driven by a destiny that is not her own, or driven to experience as a personal fate something that does not really belong to her."[92]

Though this has been my personal story of merging, I am not the only one who has experienced this. Medial women tend to carry much that does not belong to us, and to carry it deeply.

Descending

No less a scientist/theologian than Pierre Teilhard de Chardin has had the experience of descent and learned the importance of trust even amid a frightening experience. He described it in these words.

> And so, for the first time in my life perhaps (although I am supposed to meditate every day!), I took the lamp and, leaving the zone of everyday occupations and relationships where everything seems clear, I went down into my inmost self, to the deep abyss whence I feel dimly that my power of action emanates. But as I moved further and further away from the conventional certainties by which social life is superficially illuminated, I became aware that I was losing contact with myself. At each step of the descent a new person was disclosed within me of whose name I was no longer sure, and who no longer obeyed me. And when I had to stop my exploration because the path faded from beneath my steps, I found a bottomless abyss at my feet, and out of it came—arising I know not from where—the current which I dare to call *my* life.[93]

Medial women stand in good company when it comes to descent. Throughout the history of mythology and the church, the psyches of deep souls have gone into and through dark and frightening places.

Elizabeth reflected on her descent. "It seems to me that part of the journey of medial people in whatever role they find themselves, is that they have to be open to going into places beyond reason and understanding. The journey itself requires some wounding, for one must open up to everything. I have to open to the deep unconscious because fighting that pull is crazy-making for me. I suspect there has to be a period of time when the medial person knows loss and darkness. One goes through it."

Angela reflected that while she was on medication for depression, she came to understand that "depression and medication frame the distance between being here in the present and getting to where I want to go. *Being here* is not depression; rather, it's having to pull extremely hard to get to the place where I am in the space I need to be. The pull is so disruptive to my being that there needs to be some buffering outside myself. The medication allows me to make the descent while still functioning in the here and now. The alternative to making the dark, spiritual journey is somehow worse than the journey itself. The alternative of not going down would be to drive me insane. If I had to live apart from this journey, I would be crazy; I would not be me." She saw journeying into the dark night as part of what brings a person to depth and wholeness. Like all of us, Angela cannot imagine *not* making the spiritual journey through the dark places.

My own depression took the form of descent into darkness. Because I was guided in analysis, I was able to be intentional about staying there, continuing on the journey, and not harming myself. Still, I was sliding from my body and into my soul. For me, descent was what opened my consciousness to the emerging medial person that has always resided inside me. It was akin to long labor pains, but in the underworld.

This underworld was not a geographical and temporal realm, and so the language of the upper world was somehow inadequate.

Then came a dream:

I am standing on a rim above a fiery pit lined with other smaller rims down as far as I can see. Behind me is an underground parking garage, into which I know I can go and drive away from this place. I hear a voice that calls me to jump down into the fire. "Just one rim down."

And I wrote these lines in my journal the next morning:

It isn't the surface

the glitter and rush
        the commitments and pressures
                that need me to touch.

It isn't the tears
    that need to be cried
        or the rage
            or the grief
                or the childlike joy.

It's underneath these:
    the dark, fearsome void;
        the nothing and everything
            calls me to come.

"Jump down a bit further,"
    it cries out my name.
        "One more rim down.
            You're ready to come."

Who are you who summons?
    And what do you mean?
        Help me survive,
            O Voice, yet unseen.

Suddenly I found myself dropping through the underworld. Something shifted within my soul as I moved through the terror of the descent. Landing in this unknown realm was like following a dream into the night world, with all its terror and balm. Most people of the earthly realm fail to understand where I went. Those in the upper world can't understand the experience of one whose body still dwells on earth but whose soul roams beneath. I had transitioned from ego to soul, from the literal reality of upper-world perception to the archetypal images of the underworld, from the physical to the psychic perspective. I was experiencing those forces, which are divided into opposites in the upper world, now as indistinguishable. There were no longer clear differences. I was neither one thing nor the other. The visions of the world I was so carefully taught as black and white, right and wrong, were now gone. As I began to see the power and beauty of the darkness, a new self was being born, a self whose earthly mother was but a memory too bright to behold in the realm of shadows. I was pulling away from where my mother lived. I was bringing the feminine presence into the darkness of this under-realm, from which she had protected me, that landscape she most feared and had worried that I would discover and from which I would never return. I went on behalf of all women.

The Homeric Hymn to Demeter[94] touched me deeply as I coped with the rape of my own daughter and grieved a mother's grief. Later on in my own descent, I also was touched by Demeter's daughter, Persephone, as she was snatched away from picking flowers in a meadow and carried into the underworld by Hades. I, too, saw dark shadows and unfamiliar shades. However, unlike Persephone, I was not rescued by a heroic Hermes and carried into the brilliance of the upper-world sunshine with the taste of pomegranate in my mouth. I continued to learn the landscape of the underworld darkness, living there for years, gradually seeing rays of light, adjusting to brightness for a while, and retreating into the shadows. Now I continue to move between the realms: living in both simultaneously, moving from one to another. Perhaps because of this descent, I can no longer tolerate the glare of the upper world for long. My energy, my power, and my being are renewed in the dark coolness beneath. Yet I cannot stay beneath forever. I am Persephone.

Struggling with Reentry

Jungian analyst Robert Moore stated that one of the deepest problems for modern Western civilization is the lack of ritual elders, those who are rigorously trained in the geography of sacred space and who "steward the boundaries." Entering into sacred space is a process of humiliation, which must be tended, and once in sacred space, one becomes disoriented, one's reality function is suspended, and it is difficult to get out. One needs either a kick from the inside or someone from the outside to reach in and offer a hand. Such is the function of the ritual elder.[95] Such is the function of the medial woman.

While medial people may function as that hand for others, we also have a problem with making the transition when we have experiences of the depths. We need a strong ego or a centering point, not only to move amid the extraordinary experience, but we also need it to return from this realm. Joseph Campbell reminded us that we might face enormous difficulties getting back out of this sphere. "There is such a thing as *chronic liminality*—in which an individual is caught forever in limbo, unable to pull himself back together to resume a life in the world."[96] Difficulty with reentry into the ordinary realm is a corollary to becoming lost.

Medial women do have difficulty reentering the linear, physical world after experiences with the collective unconscious, the underworld, silence, the holy, or whatever realm they mediate. Getting back can be a problem for all of us.

Clelia described this with eloquence as she spoke of the trip back from a monastery at Big Sur, where she took silent retreats. The road home began winding high above the ocean and then became more condensed and urban the farther she came. She had a similar experience when she returned from a trip to Antarctica, leaving the ice, the cold space, the deep, rich water, and the penguins. She stated, "Reentry is very difficult, and I feel wounded every time I have to do it. I feel like I've cut off something essential. I promise myself that I won't cut this off again, and that I will do it differently next time. Somehow, I can't keep that promise. Reentry is a wound for me."

Elizabeth told the story of coming home from a retreat "where we meditated and had a wonderful experience right in the heart of Christmas time. Then I went home to have company that night, and I had thought my family would be a little further along with the preparations, but they were right in the midst of cleaning up. The vacuum was raging, and the stereo was pounding. That's the way my husband wants it when he's doing housework. I was in a really deep quiet place when I entered this house. I almost had to walk back out the door, but I knew I couldn't because we had people coming. I had to go forward, but I didn't want to do that. Where I *am* much of my life, where I really *want to be*, is outside of time, just plain *floating, not anywhere*. It's a place where directional motion isn't a factor at all."

When I first return from a merged state, enough creative ideas trail behind me to last years and take many forms. Sadly, I have a really hard time connecting with people who seem to be what Saint-Exupéry's Little Prince named *mushrooms*. These are the people who never smell flowers, never look at stars, never love anyone, but swell up with pride because they are busy "with matters of consequence" like adding up figures.[97]

When I return from being in some levels of the unconscious, not only do I have trouble connecting with such people, but I can no longer distinguish what is possible from what is exaggerated; night dreams send my body flying through the air. This experience is often followed by a mild bump where I come back, but I don't want to fully return to the ordinariness of the everyday world. Yet I must return. I must allow what has come from my relationship with the sacred, the creative, or the collective unconscious to have its own life, and I must continue with mine.

The difficulty in shifting from below to above has been enormous for me because I am not always sure which is which or where I am. I remember walking across my college campus in Wisconsin on a chilly March afternoon after a lecture on the complexities of Emerson. I noticed the bare trees and the gray sky reflected in an unrippled field of melted snow puddles on the campus grass. Drawn deeply into the reflections, I suddenly questioned which was the real and which was the reflected reality. I wondered if they were both real, or if the land-scape could actually be the reflection of a deeper reality. Maybe neither was real. Maybe I was going crazy. Late March was hardly my favorite time in Wisconsin.

This image of reflection speaks far more of the struggle of my soul than I realized at that youthful time. There have been several times in my life when I have felt so drawn into the reflected reality that I could not easily emerge. After one powerful guided meditation in which the guide didn't properly return us to a safe place, I was aware of living between realms for about two weeks. I need a grounded person to help me back across the boundary between the sacred and the secular. Despite, or perhaps because of, this experience and the recognition that came from it, my own call has emerged to become a grounded person of the limen for others on their passages.

Angela described her experience of disengaging or disappearing as occurring when part of her psyche was experiencing such pain that she could not stay and face it in the material world. Like me, she also at times needed several weeks to return completely. She developed a way of intentionally re-grounding by checking in with each different part of herself that she named and personified. This practice honors all the parts and gently brings them together as a whole in the world.

Jung found that he tended to stay in the other world and wrote: "I needed a point of support in 'this world,' and I may say that my family and my professional work were that to me. It was essential for me to have a normal life in the real world as a counterpoise to that strange inner world. My family and my profession remained the base to which I could always return, assuring me that I was an actually existing, ordinary person."[98]

One could also argue that sometimes a medial woman's difficulty returning from silence or powerful experiences is no different from a child's having to come inside after a summer's day of play. They just would rather not.

Becoming Lost

Some medial experiences of other realms are astonishing, breathtaking, and heady. It is easy to want to stay within them or to be unable to leave. The danger in this is becoming lost.

When I am in *participation mystique* with the sacred, with the collective unconscious, and with creativity herself, I am no longer aware of my bodily needs. Hours pass without notice; interruptions feel like hostile intrusions.

Elizabeth spoke of this as well. "One of my struggles is that I can just get lost. It's easy for me to take a step back out of my ego anytime I want to. I go to a place that's more than me, but I'm there too, and I don't totally lose myself. Coming back from the timeless, spaceless dimension of writing can be very hard. Sometimes when I go to get the kids from school after I've been writing, I feel that the other mothers look at me and think, 'Well, here comes this mother just floating in.' Here are all these people who have had a regular day. I wonder if my lostness is visible; yet, I'm much more at peace and so much happier when I've been writing. I can be really jarred too, to have to be pulled back into this world. 'Now we've got to go pick up the kids; *now* we've got to think about homework; *now* we've got to do whatever.' Oh! Very difficult!"

Kathryn also commented that she tended to lose her identity. She would just forget who she was because she felt other people's feelings so much.

Jung knew of the experience of lostness and wrote of how one encounters this in the relationship to the collective unconscious.

There I am the object of every subject, in complete reversal of my ordinary consciousness, where I am always the subject that has an object. There I am utterly one with the world, so much a part of it that I forget all too easily who I really am. "Lost in oneself" is a good way of describing this state. But this self is the world, if only a consciousness could see it. That is why we must know who we are. The unconscious no sooner touches us than we *are* it—we become unconscious of ourselves. That is the age-old danger, instinctively known and feared by primitive man.[99]

Similarly, Robert Moore wrote, "When we are in sacred space and time, we need to get a fix on a central point, some stable and unchanging reality around which we can rally our beleaguered psychological structures."[100]

Losing Our Medial Nature

In my mind, the most profound and common danger we experience as medial women is losing our medial nature.

After describing being attacked and rejected by one man whom she had helped, Kathryn commented, "People who have gifts such as mine are afraid of the things I've endured. They don't want people thinking they're ridiculous to begin with, crazy, or evil, so they don't develop or use their gifts." And yet, Kathryn quietly and courageously continued to use her gifts.

Elizabeth said that she intentionally practiced *not* being who she really was in the presence of her mother-in-law and her walking friend. This was because her reality was far away from theirs. They were so incapable of understanding it that to be in relationship with them at all, she had to be *other* than herself.

I survived childhood in a home that would have been dubious of mediality by not developing this quality of my being. In fact, I took into myself my parents' fear of that which is nonrational. As a result, I was apprehensive of my own tendencies to move toward this area. I cut off parts of my own soul—my deep wants, my needs, my own perspective and gifts—and sold my medial life in exchange for love and acceptance, a little girl's Faustian bargain. In more subtle ways, I continue to struggle with this still.

Angela said that when she got overwhelmed by external pressures from the world and was responsible for too much in the world, she was not really able to find ways to connect with her soul or that part that was unique to her. She then switched to being valued for her intelligence, efficiency, and knowledge and shifted into autopilot, losing touch with her soul.

Clelia found that she could get trapped in the upper realm. When she was a super-administrator putting her first husband through graduate school, and when she was studying for her psychology license, there was no room for her medial nature. She found that this could also happen in everyday life. She could be so burdened with the linear duties at which she excelled that she didn't have enough time for her spiritual being. She longed to be in touch with her soul without pressures; she longed to find spiritual renewal amid everyday duties instead of apart from them.

These experiences interface with what Leonard wrote. "Medial women often encounter scorn of their intuitions. Women of a gentler temperament . . . often fear to brave the attacks of more aggressive, judgmental thinkers. So, they hide their insights, keep to themselves, or fail to develop ways to express the intuitions so fundamental to their nature. Others weave their visions into poems or paintings but fear to show them to the outer world."[101]

Leonard continued, "In former times, many women hid their intuitive nature so that they would not be persecuted or tormented or ostracized as strange."[102] This is as true today as it was *in former times*. The great tragedy is when their medial qualities are lost, forgotten, or hidden from the medial woman herself.

So, I'll confess. It took me nearly 25 years since my dissertation was published to sit down and write these reflections. I was heartened to re-read a note from my advisor after my dissertation defense in which she said, "These investigations you've begun will last a lifetime. I do hope your next step will be to put them in a book."[103] I've taped that letter by my desk for courage. I have had to be intentional to let the medial voice within me do this new writing and simply toss out most of the scholarly work I had labored so hard to master all those years ago. That scholarship is still a foundation underneath all this writing, but it is no longer my voice.

I also think that my long hesitance has another dimension. The idea of releasing out into the world something this precious to me, the name by which I now call myself, is terrifying. As one wise medial woman said, "Coming out as medial is scary."

WHAT THE WORLD NEEDS NOW

Anyone who is paying attention to the world these days knows that much of what is happening is devastating. It seems like a strange time, and some even say "the end time." Human history is wracked with unpredictability, violence, tyranny, poverty, famine, pandemics, and natural disasters, each with different dimensions at different times. These ancient conditions continue to exist, along with climate change and nuclear war, which are imminent and serious threats to creation itself. It is easy to despair.

I am reminded of yet another fire dream from some years ago that has seared its image into my being. The road leading into our family cabin is a one-way twisting road that sometimes becomes miles of tangles made up of boats, trucks, trailers, RVs, motorcycles, cars, and pedestrians, all trying to move in and out. After about five miles, the road dead ends at the entrance to Desolation Valley. Along the road are homes and cabins like ours on one side and the lake on the other. The valley is made up of steep granite mountains and deep, clear lakes and is accessible only to hikers. In the dream, a wildfire is moving quickly in from the entrance of the road, and the only escape is to move up into Desolation Valley.

The other fire dreams I've had speak of the alchemical transformative quality of fire. This dream speaks of the terror, though perhaps they overlap. Some of us may watch total destruction coming our way and find that the only response is to flee into the valley of desolation.

At such a moment, my medial voice speaks to me, "You are swamped by the angst of the world's suffering, and it has become *your* angst. The porosity of your soul gives you no shield, yet it is your greatest gift and your deepest wound. Rather than discounting the power of your response and folding in under it by running into desolation, activate your unique authority."

Wolff observed that the medial woman offers the larger culture what it cannot or will not admit. She places "herself in the service of a new, perhaps just sprouting, spirit of the times."[104]

Ironically, the medial may be the most difficult structural form to discern in contemporary Western culture, just at a time when this culture stands in special need of her gifts. The medial quality, which we embody, is necessary for the creative vitality of the world and its cultures. It is food for the hungry, water for the desert. Without it, life dries up and withers.

As the Western world faces tectonic shifts, it must now find a balance to the rationality that has characterized it since the Enlightenment. It needs to be in touch with a reality beyond mechanism and materialism. It must discover a deep transformative voice amid social crisis and change. It is also essential to claim new language and guidance in the secret, profound human longing for a relationship with the divine. So, here are some of the contributions that the medial woman can make to the areas of cultural need. Plus a few stories, a poem, an active imagination, and a smile or two along the way.

Balance to Logic and Rationality

The medial woman offers much to balance the one-sided values of logic and rationality that distinguish contemporary Western culture from the rest of world history. She proclaims the unconscious contents needed for the balance and wholeness of an excessively rational culture. Few women who function through the medial archetype have been accused of being overly rational, although they may be highly effective in the culture, and most have been required to develop rationality just to get through universities. Our creative friends Tad and Noreen Guzie confirm that they are "attuned to a larger reality" and "therefore influenced by a particular kind of 'knowing'" that is not limited to reason.[105]

If a woman is a true medial, she can see what others cannot ordinarily see. However, to be useful, her task is not simply to see but also to reveal these visions to the community. To do this, she must have some access to both the rational and the sensate realm. She must see, remember, and record the visions.[106] She must learn to distinguish between what should be expressed and what should be kept silent. She must temper her revelation with judgment, timing, and method.

The phrase *dynamic feminine* describes medial qualities. The dynamic feminine is opposite to the tendency of the static masculine, which is oriented toward reasoned order or *logos* and control. Here I use the words "feminine" and "masculine" not related to gender but to psyche. Gareth Hill, a Jungian analyst in San Francisco, developed the theory of the dynamic feminine, which is "disintegrative, undirected movement toward the new, the nonrational, the playful. It is the flow of experience, vital, spontaneous, open to the unexpected, yielding and responsive to being acted upon."[107]

As one offers a balance to the rationalism of the culture, one also removes the lid that has contained feminine qualities. Helen Luke wrote that "it is time . . . for woman to turn from . . . hidden contempt for the feminine values so that she may cease to identify creativity solely with productions of thought and achievements in the outer world."[108] We "must learn how to be still without inaction, how to 'further life' without willed purpose, how to serve without demanding prestige, and how to nourish without domination."[109] These carefully modulated qualities are not limited to, but are embodied in the healthy medial woman. The medial woman's primary concern is to interpret the unconscious rather than to seek personal power or financial security. "Goals do not motivate her, and competition exhausts her."[110]

A True Story: That Department Store

Never under any circumstances do I ever go into a shopping mall on the day after Thanksgiving. Never have and never will. However, the Internet is different, and I thought I might get one special gift I needed for one special person by surfing the 'net, which I did the *night after* Thanksgiving. But I'm not a good 'net surfer; the item wasn't there, and I knew that I personally needed to get to one particular department store in the middle of a shopping center the next day if I were to stand a chance of finding this gift.

That night, however, I dreamed about *that* store. In the dream, I rode around and around in the parking lot, never getting into *that* store; I searched for *that* store; I rode the elevator 31 floors up and then back down in *that* store; I got lost in *that* store. When I woke up, I hated *that* store and never wanted to see it again, certainly not with the dreaded Saturday-After-Thanks-giving-rush into its doors. What a nightmare!

But there I was on Saturday morning at the mall with a million or so other people. I found a parking place by *that* store, took the escalator up only one floor, and walked off into exactly the department I was looking for.

But the amazing thing was that as I got off the escalator, a woman approached me and asked, "May I help you?"

"Oh, my! You are wonderful!" was all I could say.

She led me across the floor to the area I wanted, and then we realized that I needed to place an order, so she led me back to another section and patiently walked through a complex ordering process with me.

"You are wonderful," I told her again as we parted.

"You have made *my* day," she said and then began to cry. "I lost my brother the day before Thanksgiving. He was in a terrible accident. They wanted to airlift him from Modesto, but he died before they could. My boss told me not to come in today, but I needed to be here. I guess I needed to meet you. You made my day."

And she gave me a huge hug and wept in my arms. Right *there* in the middle of *that* department store on the Saturday after Thanksgiving.

And somehow, God was there too.

Somehow God does show up in the middle of the places we don't even want to go, like *that* department store. That's the irrationality of the Other.

Beyond the Mechanistic, Materialistic Worldview

First, a riddle: How are a medial woman and a computer repair process the same? (Answer to follow.)

Modern culture has a mechanistic and materialistic understanding of reality based on the assumptions of empirical sciences. To understand events from the perspective of cause and effect, one must perceive them as linear; to test material reality, one must be able to measure it. Modern culture sees time as linear and measures it by movements of the spatial bodies of the sun and moon.

The medial woman lives in two worlds at the same time. She lives and moves in this rational milieu, but she also experiences what Jungian analyst Edward Whitmont called "natural time, developmental growth time, emotional time, cosmic time, and also the 'right time,' the *kairos*, God's time, and the time that is pregnant with possibility— the moment that makes possible what other moments may not. This needs integration with the magical dimension, the sense of spatial awareness and reasoning comprehension."[111]

In this kairos realm, time and space are no longer measurable, and any moment may contain the fullness of either or both. The intersection of time and space is what Alfred North Whitehead termed an "encounter between events and the observer who has come to meet them while moving along the time scale."[112] Though all people may experience synchronicity, the medial woman, who is especially attuned to what is not seen or measured, is consciously aware of such experiences and is not quick to discount them. She knows they are a connection between the realm of mechanistic materialism and eternal moments.

Another True Story: Not Linear Hours

Some years ago, our home computer crashed. Well, it didn't really. It just wouldn't connect with any monitors we tried. So, we took it to our trusty computer guys, who had built it and added on memory. No problem. Here's the story:

"Of course, these are not linear hours," the computer guy told us as he put our ailing PC on a data-reading machine.

That was two weeks ago. No problem, except it sat "on the bench" for a week until they got to it. Eventually, they called us to get authorization for a second hour of work. "No problem," we said.

When we went to pick it up, it was being defragmented. "This is the worst fragmentation we've ever seen," they said. "Another half hour and we should be done." "No problem," we said as we headed out to do our grocery shopping.

"We need it overnight," they said when we came to pick it up. "Never seen anything like this." "No problem," we responded again.

The next day I called, "Not good news," was the response to my inquiry. "We've never seen anything like this. We may be unable to save the hard drive, but we're reading the data. The machine says that it should be ready in 25 hours. *Of course, these are not linear hours.*" "No problem, as long as you will be able to save the data," I said again. "All of it," he promised. "No problem," I replied.

So, twenty-five hours later, I called back. "How's it going?" "Big problem," he said. "Never seen anything like this in my life. Now the data reading machine says it will finish in 64 hours. We're getting some of the data. Call back next week."

Not really understanding a "not linear hour," my husband called back the next day. "Bad news," he was told. "Can't save anything. Hope you have it all backed up. [Whoops!] The technician will be here in five days, and he can tell you for sure."

May we all be open to the "not linear hours" of our lives, and may we *always* back up our data. Answer to the above riddle: They both experience nonlinear time.

Living in Kairos

As I pondered the meaning of our lost data, I also pondered the meaning of "not linear hours." I pondered the meaning of cyber-time not being linear. I pondered that while *chronos* (the ticking of time) is linear, *kairos* (the fullness of time) is not linear. I pondered the fact that memories are not linear. I pondered that true friendship is not linear. I pondered that in tragedy and trauma, time stands still. I pondered again moments in which I've experienced eternal love. I pondered that one must never take the health of one's hard drive or one's heart for granted because they can both fail when we least expect them to. While we can back up a hard drive, we can't back up a life, though we can live life to the fullest. Such fullness is not linear; it is kairos.

And I often ponder this memory, a story of someone who lived every moment to the fullness, even into her death.

Yet Another True Story: Five Minutes of Cherries

Victoria Lu was a member of our church, and over the years, she ministered more to me than I did to her.

A few days before her death, I was with Victoria and some of her family at her bedside in the skilled nursing facility. She wasn't feeling well, but some of her spirit was still very much alive.

Her dinner tray arrived with a sandwich, salad, milk, and cherries. Victoria was only willing to eat the cherries, although it was really watermelon that she wanted. So, we ordered some watermelon.

I cut the cherries and fed them to her until the watermelon arrived, and then several of us took turns feeding that to her. Then she wanted more cherries, and she wanted me to feed these to her. About this time, her sister Anna encouraged one of her own sons to feed her so I could leave. I sensed that Victoria and I needed a few more moments, so I requested "five minutes of cherries."

After the others left, Victoria and I laughed about what "five minutes of cherries" really meant, an odd way to measure cherries and an odd way to measure time. I continued to cut them and feed her, but soon she began reaching into the bowl and taking them in her fingers, dripping juice all the way to her mouth and then popping them in.

During those "five minutes of cherries," Victoria and I talked for the last time, talked about her life and death. I asked about the deep longings of her heart, as I often asked her. Sometimes in the past, her longings were that she would have time to finish up some business, or they were for the well-being of her family. This night it was a prayer, so she prayed, "Thank you for giving me everything I have ever needed or wanted. Thank you, God." As I also prayed a prayer of thanksgiving, we held each other for the last time.

In "five minutes of cherries," we both knew that we had touched the edge of eternity, and all the restlessness of life had rested. I will always remember the moment when eternity rested on a bowl of cherries.

Ability to See-Through

The archetypal psychologist James Hillman wrote: "The psyche wants to find itself by seeing-through; even more, it loves to be enlightened by seeing through itself, as if the very act of seeing-through clarified and made the soul transparent."[113]

I'm now drawn back to Spider, to whom I introduced you early in our journey together and who has helped us navigate these threads of mediality. Spider's web is multicolored, spherical, and transparent. Spider took on the color of the part of the web she was weaving, and she encouraged us to look *through* her web, not merely *at* her web. Spider knows that the very act of seeing-through the web of mediality makes our souls transparent.

Angela spoke to the sadness about the many people in our culture who look at the material reality of the web but not through the exquisite beauty on The Other Side. "I feel separated from these people. I wouldn't call them 'superficial,' because their perspective on life is real for them, but from my perspective, it's devoid of rich color and awareness. I sense that they are the ones who run the world, that there are many of them, that they talk to each other, and that they all understand *their* reality. From their perspective, I look like I'm the different one. So, I experience pain in having to expend enormous energy to fight against their impression of my not being like them, but truly I'm not. The fact is that they're the ones who don't have something, who don't know something, and who are lacking something. This difference surely is related to my mediality. My tears come from the place of being unique and different in this world and not being valued for it. They come from seeing-through."

The essence of our mediality is to see as Spider sees, to know the web and to see not only its many colors and dimensionality, but to see-through it. May we not forget.

A Story from the Neighborhood: We Are Not Other

For the first nine years of our stay in San Francisco, we lived next door to the gathering place of an unincorporated neighborhood youth group, which enjoyed lounging on our car, depositing their empties on our steps, and filling our lightwell with the smell of their marijuana. They had become for me merely a group, complete with uniforms of black pants, navy derby jackets, skateboards, and in later years, halfway dissembled cars—a group to be tolerated and ignored, a group to keep my children away from.

Perhaps because it was dark when they gathered, I never saw their faces, though I knew one of them was Jack, our next-door neighbor, the host of the group. But perhaps I would not have truly *seen* them even in the light . . . for I feared them; I resented them; I really wanted them gone.

There was one face in that neighborhood crowd outside our window one night that I *did* see: a young boy, maybe thirteen years old, holding a bottle of beer. His face was grotesquely disfigured, as though he were looking at himself in a funhouse mirror, except that he wasn't.

I looked twice because I couldn't believe what I saw:

- What accident had he experienced to leave him so deformed?
- What rejection had he known at school because of it?
- What tears had he shed when he was alone at night?
- Who held him, loved him, and suffered with him?
- What financial burdens kept his family from obtaining the help of a plastic surgeon?
- What boredom was he feeling as he waited for the school strike to end and school to begin?
- What hopes did he have for his life?
- What gentleness was revealed when he was still and alone, asleep?

Suddenly deep feeling rushed over me from some other place, and I knew that though he was not of me, he was mine:

"My son,
    My child,
        Be in peace.
            You are loved by
                The One who is Beyond Us All."

    And all Creation was new.

Creativity

Speaking of Creation, the mature medial person trusts the nature of her creativity in bridging and mediating two different realms, whatever they may be. Wolff reflected that the medial can be creative only if "she possesses the faculty of discrimination—a feeling or understanding of the specific values and limits of the conscious and the unconscious, the personal and the impersonal, of what belongs to the ego or to the surrounding environment."[114]

For the medial, sometimes the process of creativity is different from that of shaping something new. Poet Eleanor Wilner, who specialized in studying creativity, wrote that the originality of visionaries is in their "power to reformulate and creatively restructure the symbols already given."[115] She believed new vision "often requires in its carrier a special experience, one which makes [her] especially fertile ground for a recombination of old and new elements."[116] As the medial woman moves between realms and takes in and translates what is already there, her heightened awareness may be transformed into creativity.

Creativity needs us in our emptiness as much as in our fullness. I learned this when a dream visited me and gave me two crystal vessels: a long-stemmed delicate goblet and a large heavy cut-glass vase. I was told in the dream that my only task was to keep both of these vessels empty. And so, these lines:

Empty

> Empty is not nothing;
> Empty opens and receives;
> Empty anticipates and expects;
> Empty grieves and mourns;
> Empty embraces the possibilities;
> Empty hosts and has room for one more;
> Empty wanders, wonders, and waits;
> Empty energizes and offers;
> Empty happens over and over again
>   when *full* is poured out;
> Empty is the place where the leaf will come
>   on the winter tree;
> Empty is the space in my soul as it connects
>   with God, with Creativity, with You.

When we empty ourselves, we move into a land of the sacred, of the cosmic, and of connection. It is a realm beyond time and space, beyond ordinary experience, beyond yet intimately connected with matter. This is the realm that may be spoken of as "Nothingness," or that indigenous peoples have claimed as "Sacred." It may be called "extraordinary reality" as distinguished from "ordinary reality." Whatever the name, this is the realm of creativity.

Since medial women experience the heterogeneity of time and space, they can encounter both the commonplace and the extraordinary, both the secular and the holy. When she enters creative sacred space, she discovers that the inner and outer, the subject and object, the self and other become indistinguishable, and the barriers between her and the external world are broken.[117]

Mystics, medials, shamans, children, and indigenous people often move effortlessly between inner and outer realms and hold them together. Sacred space and time are filled with numinosity. This is the realm of the medial. This is indeed the realm of creativity.

Connection with the Divine

The medial woman offers her response to the contemporary cultural need for language and guidance in the secret, profound human longing for relationship with the divine. My experience is that all people long for divine wholeness, by whatever name they might give it; people long for the meaning of life, not simply to follow the rules. Surely, the quest for the *mysterium tremendum*, the awe-inspiring mystery, is an essential response to the needs of our time.

The mature medial woman has the qualities needed to guide people into relationship with this mystery. She is reverent and comfortable with symbols, rituals, worship, beauty, and art. She is a source of inspiration. Jungian analyst Nor Hall, another medial woman accompanying us on our journey, spoke of the medial as being *the spirit of clarification.* "A woman who experiences herself as a medium knows that she has not invented her visions but that she is capable of revealing hidden sources, showing people what they may already know but have hidden or never recognized."[118] And Jungian analyst Helen Luke wrote that she honors the mystery and essential value of the individual secret, without which one loses contact with the soul.[119]

The language of the soul and the language of logos rationality are two completely different languages, and both are essential. Luke reminded us that "when great symbols lose their content and their meaning for us, we are in danger of losing our souls."[120] The medial woman naturally knows the language of soul, that of deep reality, which is expressed in images and symbolism. Yet, as de Castillejo asserted, she also must know "the difference between the world of images and the world of everyday if she is to stand in the middle and mediate one to the other."[121] The effective medial woman listens with discrimination, not only to what is beyond but also to what is within.

This language is the language of soul, which we must each learn to interpret.

The divine often shows up right in our midst, and how easily we can miss it. I discovered this on the last day of classes in my graduate program. Reading and papers, lectures and presentations, late-night discussions, written and oral comprehensives, dissertation planning and concept papers: all this had been the "stuff" of my life in graduate school for the past three years. In a surprising way, everything came together during an evening family picnic for students, staff, and their families on the lovely campus during the last week of classes.

Baptism of Roses

She picks her way carefully down the path, seemingly alone, blonde ringlets bouncing, and she waves as though we were longtime friends. How many years has it been since I've talked, really talked, to a two-year-old? "Hi, what's your name?" I say as I sit down on my heels under the low oak tree branch that swings across the trail alongside the Lecture Hall. "Talley," she answers. "I'm so glad to meet you. My name's Bobbie." "Bobbie," she responds. "Are you alone?" I ask. "No, Talley and Sarah." She turns up the path and announces to all the world and God, "Bobbie's here! Bobbie's here!" A young woman gently moves toward us on the trail. "Bobbie's here!" Talley continues. I introduce myself to the woman and learn that she is Talley's mother, Sarah; we speak briefly, all the while Talley is saying to her, "Bobbie's here." As we part, she asks my name again, and after I tell her, Sarah says, "Oh, Talley *was* trying to introduce you."

As the evening barbecue progresses, I meet Rebecca, Anna, and Lucy, three beautiful, dark children from Third-World countries who have just moved from the East Coast so their mother can be one of our faculty members. We talk and tease for a few minutes, and then they are off to dinner and other adventures, as am I.

Following dinner, I head down yet another trail with the adults for the evening's program when suddenly I feel two small arms around my waist and hear the words, "Where have you been? I've been looking for you. I want to put roses on your head." It is Anna. "I'll come," I respond. What else could I possibly want in the middle of a strenuous week of classes than roses on my head? I follow her down another path as she races on ahead.

However, I am waylaid as I come upon Talley's five-year-old brother, Stephen, squatting by a hole in an oak tree's roots. "Who do you suppose lives here?" he asks as he peers into the hole, proving that five-year-olds can indeed be archetypalists. We ponder the question as we sit and look together; he holds a long strand of grass, trying to tickle out who is the Who who lives here.

Suddenly over my head falls a shower of colored petals. I've never been baptized with roses, but their gentle weight carries the power of the spirit as fully as the hands of ordaining bishops, and the laugh that goes with them arises from its own center of authority in the playful child. And then she is off, and Stephen with her.

Again, I stand in the middle of the path, wondering whether to go with the circle of adults and hear the telling of a creation myth or to follow the children who are in the act of creating. I choose the children. Lucy tickles me with a frond. Anna settles in with me on the step for a moment now and then to share about her life. More rose petals appear on my shoulders, and their thorns also appear in a small bleeding finger, which needs a kiss, a napkin to wrap up in, and a gentle squeeze.

Talley gives me two rocks, which I tell her I will put into my rock collection. "Stephen broke his," she informs me. "His rock collection," she adds as she races off again.

Then as always, night falls; the children leave to go to their homes and beds, as do I, with the weight of two small rocks in my pocket, the weight of the baptism of roses still fresh on my head, and the awareness of having been visited by small angels. How my soul has needed the play of angels.

Is this not our challenge: To see, learn, and experience all that we can from many points of view, and, while honoring different expressions, to be bold enough to identify and call by name God's presence in the midst, however it shows up?

Our Times Cry Out for the Transformative Voice

Present Western culture needs a deep transformative voice amid social crisis and change, and the medial woman is often this voice. It is she who sees through the web. It is she who picks up what goes on beneath the surface of a group or society and voices it. It is she who senses what is happening in the environment, though she may not even be aware of it. It is she who moves with ease through the distortions of measured time and space. It is she who gives voice to the gods and goddesses and to the deepest longings of human nature.

"Where human order falters, the gods intervene,"[122] penned Eleanor Wilner. The medial woman is one who points to the gods as they move into the human realm. What emerges in crisis "is the response of an innate integrative function, a kind of 'voice of human nature.' . . . The voice of this partly unconscious life-affirming and ordering force is loudest when integrity is most deeply threatened, when the conflicting forces in men [sic] and society are most at odds and the need for synthesis most acute."[123]

To be a transformative voice, the medial woman needs to have a flexible and vigorous ego. With the ego intact, she can relate to the unconscious rather than being swamped by it. "In Jung's language, the ego is the place where we meet the Self, the center of the whole psyche," Ann Ulanov wrote. One needs the ego to receive, digest, and channel the archetypal images that wash in. Perhaps even more significantly, "the ego is needed to reach that indefinable core that we call the soul life of a person." When this happens, "each reaches to that precious I-ness in other persons."[124] Or as the great Jewish theologian Martin Buber described the meeting of one with another in love, "I become through my relation to the Thou; as I become I, I say *Thou*. All real living is meeting."[125]

Our times cry out for the transformative voices of medial women. Without these, life is likely unidimensional, unidirectional, achievement-oriented, competitive, driven by cause and effect, rigid, competitive, contained, and a bit flat. The gifts medials introduce into this culture bring a new awareness of other realms and realities, which are organic, circular, multidirectional in movement, and honor the moment. The medial woman offers a mindfulness that respects the gifts of each, listens to the meaning of imagery, symbolism, and symptom, and ritualizes truth through art and community experience. She transmits unseen reality to a world in great need. She brings an awareness that shows flexibility, openness, variety, mystery, and energy, and is in relationship with the divine by whatever name it takes. She is vulnerable, and she is powerful.

The strength that medial women have built up and sustained through their wounding can be converted into power, authority, and service as they become leaders in a new era that will honor a broader range of archetypal expressions.

I think of the power and the pain of the most vulnerable among us, the newborn baby. The world rejoices as it breaks through into life with all its raw potential, ready to move forth with cries out into the universe. Naming the medial woman is the act of birthing her. May the world rejoice in now seeing that which has been hidden before its very eyes and is now known.

CONCLUSION

Protecting Our Hearts

This is one last story from when my daughter Alisa (also a medial woman) was perhaps three years old. She had a high fever. As I asked how she felt, she responded in a way that I have carried in my soul all these years.

> "My eyelashes hurt; my ankles hurt; my hair hurts; my cheeks hurt."
> When I tried to sum it all up by saying, "It sounds as though everything hurts," she responded, "Everything hurts but my heart."
> I held her close and thought a mother's thought, "Alisa, may it always be so."

I am reminded of this story as I listen to the world. So many people, institutions, countries, and the Earth, herself, are hurting deeply—hurting to the eyelashes, to the ankles, to the hair, and to the cheeks. Fever ravishes our society and leaves us feeling broken.

When everything seems to hurt, I hope that with Alisa, we too can say, "Everything hurts but my heart." Our hearts are much more than heavy-duty mechanical pumps separating health from sickness, and life from death. Through the eyes of poets over the years, the heart has come to mean feeling, passion, intuition, motivation, and the center of being and faith.

When John Wesley, the founder of Methodism, and his friends met, they didn't banter a "Hiya, how's it going?" Rather they inquired of each other, "Is it right with your heart?"

Jesus left his disciples with these words:

> Peace, I leave with you; my peace I give to you. I do not give
> to you as the world gives. Do not let your *hearts* be troubled,
> and do not be afraid.[126]

The psalmist prayed:

> Search me, O God, and know my *heart*.
> Test me and know my anxious thoughts![127]

When so much seems to hurt, protect your heart. Guard it, tend
it, love it. Be gentle with that which is at the center of your being. And
perhaps we together can become the heart of our hurting communi-
ties, being called with new courage and boldness to stand amidst the
hungry and the poor, the despairing and the angry, with constancy,
love, and hope. May we be called with greater assurance to live our
lives, our truths, our mediality, each in her unique way.

Final Words from Toni Wolff

As I did at the beginning, I now at the ending call upon the presence of Toni Wolff. This time I don't seek the wisdom from her
psychological sophistication, her influence, or her intellectual writing.
Rather, this comes from an essay she wrote as a young woman before
she ever met Jung and before she abandoned her creative writing.
Wolff penned, "The poet sees the insoluble mystery, and with his
harp, sings of the sorrows and joys of every human destiny."[128] As I
invite her to expand this reflection, I now hear her say:

> The medial sees the insoluble mystery,
> and with her harp sings of the sorrows and joys of
> every human destiny.

PRAYER OF WOMEN AT THE LIMEN

Deep Mystery, Divine Spirit, Sacred Other, Source of All, Ground of
Being, God,
    You, beyond name, concepts, or words,
        You, to which medial women are connected,
            we lift this prayer:

May our limen be the edge of your hand.
Hold us in your open palm:
    not too tightly,
        that we might be crushed;
    not too lightly,
        that we might slip off.

May we find
    courage in the darkness that we travel
        discernment in what is ours to know and carry
            wisdom to leave what is not ours behind
                balance between the one foot on this side
                and the one foot on the other.

May our culture grow from encasement to the old ways
    through the chaos of disruption into new forms
        that are permeable enough to embrace ancient wisdom
        as well as new ways of being.

May there be room for our gifts
    among the gifts of those many others: so very different
    all of which are needed

so that we can live into the fullness of our beings
so that we can be heard
amidst clatter and clutter.

May we find respect among other women
Those who carry swords
Those who carry babies
Those who carry hearts
As we carry insights and hidden truths.

While we acknowledge our wounds,
may they not create of us victims.

While we claim our gifts,
may they not create in us arrogance.

We are becoming ever more the Self we have been from birth.
Use us in service to the greater whole.
May our being make a difference in Creation.

So May It Be

GRATITUDE

With thanks beyond words to the midwives of this work:

Betty De Shong Meador, Jungian analyst, scholar, and the advisor to my dissertation, who was the first to tell me that "these investigations you have begun will last a life-time. I do hope your next step will be to put them into a book."

Naomi Lowinsky, Jungian analyst and published poet, my writing consultant and teacher, who patiently and with deep understanding guided me through twelve drafts to something totally new and just seemed to understand what both the work and I needed at the moment.

Jennifer Leigh Selig, my publisher at Mandorla, who is filled with grace, knowledge and creativity, and who has brought to life what feels like another child of mine.

With deep appreciation to those who have come out of the shadows and journeyed with me:

Angela, Clelia, Elizabeth, and Kathryn, as well as the many writers whose wisdom I have used along the way, and who are named in the bibliography.

With deep thanks to:

Carl Culberson, Presbyterian minister and Jungian analyst, who guided my medial soul from the shadows in our many years of work together, and whom I believe is cheering this writing on from The Other Side, where he now resides.

With great gratitude to those medial women who have stood shoulder to shoulder to me in this writing process, reviewed the manuscript, and offered gentle critique and enthusiastic endorsement:

Katherine Boyle, Jane Cohn, Mary Culberson, Karen Dolamanisth, Nesita Kwan, Sharon Thornton

and to my forever college friend, Nick Vogel, (a brilliant lawyer, clearly not a medial woman), for his curiosity about this book from the beginning and for his careful editing and comments.

Finally, with unending gratitude for my Beloved husband, Richard Corson, who has been with me through the life process of discovery, of questioning, of pain and doubt, of joy and hope, of the call to give birth to this volume. His hand guided me as I stepped out of the shadows. He understands, loves, and supports me always.

ABOUT THE AUTHOR

Roberta Bassett Corson is retired as a clinical depth psychologist and United Methodist clergy. She was raised in Palo Alto, CA and lives in Saratoga, CA. She holds a B.A. in English Literature from Lawrence University, a M.Div. from Pacific School of Religion, and a Ph.D. from Pacifica Graduate Institute. She has been married for over 50 years and is mother of two and grandmother of two. As a medial woman who is aware of the many women like her who long to be called by name, she continues to explore the dimensions of mediality with the hope that these women can be named and known. They are not alone.

Visit Roberta Corson at www.robertabcorson.com

BIBLIOGRAPHY

Aeschylus. (2011). Agamemnon. *The complete Aeschylus: Volume 1* (P. Burian & A. Shapiro Ed. & Trans.). Oxford University Press. (Original work written 5th century B.C.E.)

Buber, M. (1957). *I and Thou.* (R.G. Smith, Trans.). Charles Scribner's Sons.

Corson, R. (1998) *The wounds of medial women in contemporary Western culture.* [Unpublished doctoral dissertation. Pacifica Graduate Institute]

Dallett, J. (1986). Artist, analyst, shaman, thief. *Psychological Perspectives, 17*(1), 71-83.

de Castillejo, I.C. (1973). *Knowing woman: A feminine psychology.* Harper and Row.

_____ (1983). Woman as mediator. In M. Tuby (Ed.), *In the Wake of Jung: A Selection from Harvest* (pp. 53-56). Coventure Ltd.

de Saint-Exupéry, A. (1975). *The little prince.* (K. Woods, Trans.). Scholastic Book Services.

Fletcher, S. (2010) *The highland witch.* W. W. Norton and Company.

Goerlick, K. (1989). Rapprochement between the arts and psychotherapies: Metaphor as mediator. *The Arts in Psychotherapy: An International Journal, 16*(3). 149-156.

Guzie, T. & Guzie, N. (1986). *About men & women: How your "great story" shapes your destiny.* Paulist Press.

Healy, N. S. (2017). *Toni Wolff & C.G. Jung: A collaboration.* Tiberius Press.

Hall, N. (1980). *The moon and the virgin: Reflections on the archetypal feminine.* Harper & Row.

Hill, G.S. (1987). March. *Masculine and feminine.* [Paper presented at the public program at the C.G. Jung Institute of San Francisco]

Hillman, J. (1975). *Re-visioning psychology*. Harper Perennial.

Homer. (2020). *Demeter and Persephone: Homeric Hymn Number Two*. https://chs.harvard.edu/primary-source/homeric-hymn-to-demeter-sb/ (Original work written ca. 8th century B.C.E.)

Jones, R.K. (2019, May, 29). Grief transformation; cocoons and butterflies. *Chaplain Resources*. https://www.chaplainusa.org/robert-jones-journal/grief-transformation-cocoons-and-butterflies

Jung, C.G. (1953). *The collected works of C.G. Jung* (Vol. 7). (R. F. C. Hull, Trans.)/ Princeton University Press. (Original work published in 1917)

_____ (1959). *The collected works of C.G. Jung* (Vol. 9i). (R. F. C. Hull, Trans.). Princeton University Press. (Original work published in 1934)

_____ (1961). *Memories, dreams, and reflections*. (A. Jaffe, Ed). (R. & C. Winston Trans.). Vintage Books.

Kübler-Ross, E. (1997). *The wheel of life: A memoir of living and dying*. Simon & Schuster, Touchstone.

Leonard, L.S. (1993). *Meeting the madwoman: An inner challenge for feminine spirit*. Bantam.

Luke, H.M. (1981). *Woman, earth and spirit: The feminine in symbol and myth*. Crossroad.

_____ (1993). *Kaleidoscope: The way of woman and other essays*. Morning Light Press.

Mattoon, M.A. (1981). *Jungian psychology in perspective*. The Free Press.

Moore, R. (1984, April). *The nature of sacred space*. Taped lecture #150. The Jung Institute of Chicago.

Moore, R. & Gillette, D. (1993). *The magician within: Accessing the shaman in the male psyche*. William Morrow and Company.

Pearson, C.S. (1991). *Awakening the heroes within: Twelve archetypes to help us find ourselves and transform our world*. HarperSanFrancisco.

Rand, H. (2020). *Everything you wanted to know about the afterlife but were afraid to ask*. Atria Paperback.

Rilke, R.M. (1984). The Duino elegies: The first elegy. (Unpublished translation by G. Heilek)

Shapira, L.L. (1988). *The Cassandra complex: Living with disbelief: A modern perspective on hysteria*. Inner City Books.

Sherlock, P.K. (1980) *The relationship of Wolff's archetypal feminine images to time orientation and related psychological variables*. [Unpublished doctoral dissertation. Pacific Graduate School of Psychology]

_____ (1984). The feminine Q-set: New research on Wolff's feminine images and theories. *Journal of Analytical Psychology, 29*, 187-199.

Stein, M. (1998). *Jung's map of the soul: An introduction.* Open Court.

Teilhard de Chardin, P. (1960). *The divine milieu.* Harper & Row.

Tillich, P. (1967). *Systematic theology: Three volumes in one* (Vol. I). Harper & Row.

_____ (1952). *The courage to be.* Yale University Press.

_____ (1963). *The eternal now.* Chapter 11. Scribner Book Company.

Ulanov, A. (1971). *The feminine in Jungian psychology and in Christian theology.* Northwestern University.

_____ (1988). *The wisdom of the psyche.* Cowley.

_____ (1981). *Receiving woman: Studies in the psychology and theology of the feminine.* The Westminster Press.

Ulanov, A. and B. (1987). *The witch and the clown: Two archetypes of human sexuality.* Chiron.

Urrea, L.A. (2006). *The hummingbird's daughter.* Little, Brown and Company.

Van der Leeuw, G. (1964) *Religion: In essence and manifestation.* (J. E Turner, Trans.). Princeton University Press.

von Franz, M-L. (1980). *Alchemy.* Inner City Books.

Whitmont, E. (1976). Momentum of man: The cultural evolution of the masculine and feminine. *Quadrant, 9*(1), 3-15.

_____ (1969). *The symbolic quest: Basic concepts of analytical psychology.* Princeton University Press.

Wilner, E. (1975). *Gathering the winds: Visionary imagination and radical transformation of self and society.* The Johns Hopkins University Press.

Wolff, T. (1934). *Goethe abend.* [Lecture presented to the Psychologischer Club Zurich, March 19, 1932. Psychologischer Club Zurich library archives, Zurich]

_____ (1941). A few thoughts on the process of individuation in women. *Spring.* 81-103. [Published from a lecture by Toni Wolff to the Psychological Club in Zurich, 1934]

_____ (1956). *Structural forms of the feminine psyche.* (P. Watzlawik, Trans.). Privately printed for the Students Association, C.G. Jung Institute, Zurich. (Original work published in 1951)

_____ (1995). Structural forms of the feminine psyche. (G. Jacobson, Trans.). *Psychological Perspectives, 31*, 77-90. (Original work published in 1951)

Wordsworth, W. (1804). *Ode: Intimations of immortality.* https://www.poetryfoundation.org/poems/45536/ode-intimations-of-immortality-from-recollections-of-early-childhood

ENDNOTES

[1] R.M. Rilke. (1923). *The Duino elegies: First Elegy.* (unpublished Trans. by G. Heilek).

[2] The work of N.S. Healy. *Toni Wolff & C.G. Jung.* 2017, offers many insights into the person, relationships, and contributions of Toni Wolff.

[3] Wolff developed a theory that she named *The Structural Forms of the Feminine Psyche,* in which she explored the nature of women's psychological being. She presented her emerging ideas in a lecture, which she delivered to the Psychological Club in Zurich in 1934 and was published in 1941. She then published a more condensed and updated version in an essay in 1951, and I shall use the 1995 translation of the essay in these reflections. The references are as follows:

- T. Wolff. (1941). "A few thoughts on the process of individuation in women." *Spring,* 81. (Published from a paper read by Toni Wolff to the Psychological Club in Zurich May, 1934).

- T. Wolff. (1956). *Structural forms of the feminine psyche.* P. Watzlawik, Trans. (Zürich, Switzerland: Privately printed for the Students Association, C.G. Jung Institute, 1956, Original essay published in 1951).

- T. Wolff. (1995). Structural forms of the feminine psyche. (G. Jacobson, Trans.) *Psychological Perspectives, 31,* 77-90. (Original work published in 1951).

[4] M. Stein (1998). *Jung's Map of the Soul.* 88. (Kindle edition).

[5] A. & B. Ulanov. (1987). 305.

[6] T. Wolff. (1956/1951). 80.

[7] T. Wolff. (1995/1951). 81.

[8] Ibid., 80.

[9] Ibid., 80.

[10] Ibid., 83.

[11] T. Wolff. (1995/1951). 86.

[12] I.C. de Castillejo. (1983). 56.

[13] Ibid., 58.

[14] P. K. Sherlock (1984). 194.

[15] L. Leonard. (1993). 242-245.

[16] T. Guzie & N. Guzie. (1986). 85.

[17] I.C. de Castillejo. (1983). 63.

[18] E. Whitmont. (1969). 181.

[19] M. Mattoon. (1981). 92.

[20] H. Luke. (1992). 170.

[21] L. Leonard. (1993). 240-279.

[22] T. Guzie & N. Guzie. (1086). 24-28.

[23] A. Ulanov. (1971). 207-209.

[24] The Gospel of Matthew 26:36 ff. (New International Version).

[25] The Gospel of Matthew 27:46 (New International Version).

[26] P. Tillich. (1967).

[27] P. Tillich. (1952).

[28] P. Tillich. (1963). Chapter 11.

[29] John 20:17

[30] P. K. Sherlock. (1984).

[31] I.C. de Castillejo. (1983). 62-63.

[32] H. Rand. (2020). 14-15.

[33] M-L. von Franz. (1980). 49-50.

[34] R. Romanyshyn. (1993). (unpublished lecture, Pacifica Graduate Institute).

[35] The Gospel of John 19:38-42.

[36] M-L. von Franz. (1980). 75.

[37] W. Wordsworth. (1804). *Ode: Intimations of Immortality*.

[38] T. Wolff. (1941/1934). 96.

[39] T. Wolff. (1941/1934). 103.

[40] Author unknown. Commonly attributed incorrectly to William Blake (1790). *The Marriage of Heaven and Hell*.

[41] T. Wolff. (1995/1951). 86.

[42] I.C. de Castillejo. (1983). 65.

[43] T. Guzie & N. Guzie. (1986). 24.

[44] A. Akhmatova as quoted in L. Leonard. (1993). 261.

[45] K. Goerlick. (1989) 152.

[46] http://jungcurrents.com/helen-preiswerk

[47] Exodus 3:5.

[48] E. Kubler-Ross. (1997). 76.

[49] R.K. Jones (2019). https://www.chaplainusa.org/robert-jones-journal/grief-transformation-cocoons-and-butterflies.

[50] A. Ulanov. (1988). 19.

[51] C.G. Jung. (1953). [CW 7, para. 103]. 66.

[52] H. Luke. (1992). 170.

[53] L. Leonard. (1993). 278-279.

[54] T. Moore. (1994). (unpublished lecture, Pacifica Graduate Institute).

[55] T. Guzie & N. Guzie. (1986). 50.

[56] A. Ulanov. (1988). 19.

[57] Steven Aizenstat. (1993). (personal communication).

[58] T. Moore. (1994). (unpublished lecture, Pacifica Graduate Institute).

[59] A. Ulanov. (1988). 19.

[60] Leonard. (1993). 254.

[61] Ibid., *276*.

[62] Ibid., *258*.

[63] Ibid., *278*.

[64] J. Dallett. (1986). 76.

[65] Pearson. (1991). 197.

[66] T. Wolff. (1995/1951). 85.

[67] I.C. de Castillejo. (1983). 63

[68] A. Ulanov. (1971). 210.

[69] T. Wolff. (1995/1951). 87.

[70] Ibid., 80.

[71] W. Wordsworth. 1807.

[72] P.K. Sherlock (1980). 37.

[73] A. Ulanov. (1971). 210.

[74] J. Dallett. (1986). 76.

[75] T. Guzie & N. Guzie (1986). 25.

[76] L. Leonard. (1993). 243.

[77] J. Dallett. (1986). 76.

[78] Ibid., 82.

[79] T. Wolff. (1951/1955). 87.

[80] Aeschylus. (2011/5th century B.C.E.).

[81] I.C. de Castillejo. (1983). 63.

[82] L. Leonard. (1993). 246.

[83] Peter Byrne, S. J. (1975).

[84] I.C. de Castillejo. (1983). 64.

[85] L. Leonard. (1993). 244.

[86] T. Wolff. (1995/1951). 86.

[87] L. Leonard. (1993). 277.

[88] L. L. Shapira. (1989). 65.

[89] L. Leonard, (1993). 243-244.

[90] A. Ulanov. (1981). 88.

[91] E. Wilner. (1975). 12.

[92] A. Ulanov. (1971). 209.

[93] P. Teilhard de Chardin. (1960). 48.

Pierre Teilhard de Chardin strikes me as a medial man. As a pale-ontologist and a deep theological thinker, he bridged the material/scientific and the spiritual worlds. His writing was forbidden to be published by the Roman Catholic Church at the time it was written, since he rejected the literal interpretation of the Genesis story of creation. He developed a complex theory of cosmic theology based on evolution and is now credited with bringing theology into the contemporary world. He told friends that he hoped he would die on Easter, and a month later on Easter evening after a vigorous day, he had a massive heart attack and died.

[94] Homer. (2020/ca. 8th century B.C.E.).

[95] R. Moore. (1984).

[96] J. Campbell (quoted in R. Moore). 133.

[97] A. de Saint-Exupéry. (1975). 29.

[98] C.G. Jung. (1961). 189.

[99] C.G. Jung. (1959). [CW 9i, para. 46-47]. 22.

[100] R. Moore. (1993). 129.

[101] L. Leonard (1993). 242.

[102] L. Leonard. (1993). 245.

[103] Betty Meador. (personal correspondence). 1998.

[104] T. Wolff. (1995/1951). 87.

[105] T. Guzie & N. Guzie. (1983). 25.

[106] L. Leonard. (1993). 276.

[107] G. Hill. (1987). 7.

[108] H. Luke. (1981). 3.

[109] Ibid., 12.

[110] T. Guzie & N. Guzie. (1983). 25.

[111] E. Whitmont. (1976). 11.

[112] A.N. Whitehead (quoted in Whitmont). 11.

[113] J. Hillman. (1985). 123.

[114] T. Wolff. (1995/1951). 87.

[115] E. Wilner. (1975). 21.

[116] Ibid., 27.

[117] G. van der Leeuw. (1964). 493.

[118] N. Hall. (1980). 169.

[119] H. Luke. (1981). 23-24.

[120] Ibid., 41.

[121] I.C. de Castillejo, (1983), 63.

[122] E. Wilner. (1975). 33.

[123] Ibid., 5.

[124] A. Ulanov. (1988). 2-3.

[125] M. Buber. (1957). 11.

[126] John 14:27 (New International Version).

[127] Psalm 139:23 (New International Version).

[128] T. Wolff. "Goethe Abend." 5, 10.

9 781950 186457